True Life in God

Vassula

Volume Five

(Notebooks 54-58)

Published by

♡ ♡
Trinitas™

Declaration

The decree of the Congregation for the Propagation of the Faith, A.A.S. 58, 1186 (approved by Pope Paul VI on October 14, 1966) states that the Nihil Obstat and Imprimatur are no longer required on publications that deal with private revelations, provided they contain nothing contrary to faith and morals.

The publisher wishes to manifest unconditional submission to the final and official judgement of the Magisterium of the Church.

True Life in God

Vassula

Volume Five

(Notebooks 54-58)

Second printing 11-92 (Cover image changed.)

Published by

Trinitas™

P.O. Box 475
Independence, Missouri, USA 64051
Phone (816) 254-4489

For further information direct all inquires to Trinitas.

Cover photo: from Agamian Portrait, courtesy of Holy Shroud Guild.

Printed in United States of America.

Also available in Spanish, French, Italian, German. Translations in progress include Greek, Danish, Russian, Portuguese, and Japanese. For information contact Trinitas.

Table of Contents

Vassula

Welcome

To the praise of Jesus and Mary

In reading the messages, always read Volume One first and follow the order of the books so that you become immersed in God's Love for you.

Jesus asked me to tell you to always take my name, Vassula, out of the messages and replace it with your own name.

I really must express here my gratitude to my family, my spiritual director, and all my faithful friends who have made the preparation of this book possible.

I want to mention Father René Laurentin, Sr. Lucy Rooney, Father Bob Faricy, Father Michael O'Carroll, Tony Hickey, Pat Callahan, Tom Austin, and everyone who promotes and helps distribute these messages. I bless the Lord and thank Him for the ears that heard His Cry of Love from His Cross and now, touched, become His mouthpieces broadcasting this Cry of Love.

The text presented in this volume is the original English. At my request, there have been some abbreviations and additions which were necessary either due to the personal nature of a message or to clarify the sense of certain passages.

Vassula

Previous Volume Synopsis

True Life In God
Volume One

1) **Notebooks 1-16**
2) *A Note to the Reader* by Lucy Rooney, SND and Robert Faricy, SJ
3) *Foreword* by Patrick de Laubier, Professor, University of Geneva; University of Fribourg, Switzerland
4) *Introduction* by Fr. René Laurentin
   - Nine pages of interviews with Vassula.
   - A graphological analysis by handwriting expert J.A. Munier.
   - Excerpts from a speech by Fr. Don Gobbi, of the Marian Movement.
5) *A Book of Prayer* by Vladimir Zielinski, Russian Orthodox Theologian

True Life In God
Volume Two

1) **Notebooks 17-28**
2) *Introduction* by Fr. James Fannan, Vassula's Spiritual Director through April, 1991
3) *Foreword* by Fr. Michael O'Carroll, Vassula's Spiritual Director
4) *Presentation* by Fr. René Laurentin

True Life In God
Volume Three

1) **Notebooks 29-41**
2) *Introduction* by Tony Hickey, Director, Manchester Medjugorje Center, Manchester England

True Life In God
Volume Four

1) **Notebooks 42-53**
2) *Introduction* by Fr. Michael O'Carroll, Vassula's Spiritual Director

"A Spiritual Echo of Unity"

Vassula Ryden

Address to the Ecumenical Conference of the World Council of Churches

The following is a transcript of Vassula Ryden's address to the Ecumenical Conference of the World Council of Churches, held during Unity Week, January 23, 1992, in the Ecumenical Center, Geneva, Switzerland.

Ms. Vassula Ryden is a voice of spirituality and unity. She speaks to all Christians, Orthodox, Catholics, and Protestants, transmitting a message of peace love, and unity: "May they all be one," by the grace of the Holy Spirit. Many who have listened to the message have found it to be a deep source of inspiration. She has been invited by interested collegues.
- from the material introducing Vassula's talk

I will read you a small introduction about myself, and then later on I will read you a few messages of unity.

I'm baptized Greek Orthodox, of Greek parents, and we are all born in Egypt. My husband is Swedish, and a Lutheran. I have two sons and I am a housewife. I was never taught any catechism, let alone any theology. I abandoned the practice of my faith entirely, especially when I was married. I had not heard that the Lord can give us extraordinary favors like locutions and intellectual visions, or lights infused into the intellect.

One day, when I least expected it, God came suddenly upon me and seized me. It was at the end of November, 1985. That part of the month I was preparing a painting exhibition. I was playing tennis from morning till night (whenever they wanted Vassula they could get her at the tennis court), and I was modeling clothes.

God was very far from me. When God approached me, He sent first my guardian angel. He came to me while I was preparing a grocery list. He presented himself and gave me Daniel as his name. As simple as that! You can imagine my surprise and my joy. Later on, I found out I could communicate with my angel. I heard his voice in my heart and I wrote down, as under dictation. My mere thought, which I also wrote down, was answered. So everything began in this style.

The first day, when my husband learned about it, it never occurred to me that he would doubt. He knew that I was in my normal mind. I wasn't somebody to invent such a thing. He just believed. The Old Testament frequently shows us angels used by God, not only as messengers, but as instruments, too.

After a week, my angel asked me to read the Bible, and I had none at home, so he told me to go and fetch one. I did, and when I opened it to read, like he told me to do, I opened to the psalms, and I couldn't understand anything, although it was English. That was God, trying to tell me I was blind and it is all dark around me, and therefore I can't understand what I am saying.

The angel gave me a purification He started to show me all the sins I had not repented in a very special way, very special, because, it was like God sees our sins, and not like we see them. And there's a big difference. I suffered a lot because I hated myself, and I hated everything I had been doing.

My angel asked me to go over to the seminary, which happened to be opposite our house, in Bangladesh. I found a priest, and I revealed my writings, and told him everything. He was stunned, and he didn't believe me. I was shattered because, in my ignorance, I really thought he would believe me, since he was dealing, day and night, with God and angels. From then on, he treated me as one who is mentally disturbed. He then sent me to another priest who concluded that I was dealing with Satan. So I ended up with one thinking that I'm mad and the other one thinking that I'm satanic.

After a few weeks, instead of the regular visit of my angel, it was the Lord Himself that visited me. In the state I was, I did not leap with surprise. Since I did not know the Lord, I considered everybody who descended from heaven equal. The first thing the Lord said was "I, God, love you. Love me." Then He asked me to say the Our Father to Him.

A few days later, Jesus asked me a question. He said, "Which house is more important, your house or my house?" I said, "Your house, Lord." So He blessed me. Then He said, "My house is in ruin. Renew my house." I almost cried, because I said, "How? How can I do any thing? I don't know anything about the church. And I don't know anything about catechism, absolutely nothing. You're asking something I cannot do."

In the meantime, the first priest, who thought I was mentally disturbed, started to suspect that it might all be from God, and said, "Vassula, I feel very sorry for you, because God does not come to anyone in such a way, giving so many graces, without wanting something."

True. One day Jesus asked me, "Would you like to serve me?" And I did not answer because I was frightened. Since everything was being written down, I lifted my hand, because I did not want this to be written down. It really scared me. I did not know what God would ask of me. I thought maybe He might tell me to leave my family and run to be a Carmelite. I wasn't ready. So, I pushed Him away. But I couldn't be quiet the whole day and the whole night because He said, just after that, "I can abide in you, in spite of your awesome weak-

ness." Then I felt very, very, sorry, and so I decided to plunge into darkness more or less. The next day, I came up with His own question, and I said, "Would you like me to serve you?" So He said, "I will raise you to appease my justice. I will raise you to delight my soul. You have no merits, none at all, but I favored you, in spite of your wretchedness, for my loyalty and my gentleness are without measure."

One day the Lord gave me a vision of three iron bars standing near each other. The vision was pursuing me all morning. Then He infused in me a light to understand its meaning, and when I understood that they represented the Catholics, Protestants, and Orthodox Churches I panicked, and I said, "No, I don't want to be involved in these things. It was nice to be just You and me, but now that You're going to talk about churches. I don't want to be involved in these messages. Keep me out of this. At any rate, I have no idea of the churches programs. Take someone who knows all these things, and has authority, and who's respected by the church."

But Jesus said, "I shall form you and teach you." I said, "But I know nothing at all." And He said, "I have chosen you because you have no authority, and you are nothing. Through your nothingness, I will reveal My Greatness. Through your misery, I will show My mercy. And through your frailty, My strength. Remain nothing, so that I may be everything. I do not want a rival. Die to yourself, so that My Spirit breathes in you. Efface yourself so that only I may be seen. I have chosen you, unfit for this task, helpless and small, without prestige, to manifest, through you, My Passionate Love. My church needs a renewal. I have come to consolidate My Church, so allow Me to use you."

I was called under Divine dictation every day. The Lord always asks my permission, "Allow Me to use your hand, allow Me to use your time." He never forced me. With my permission He started to detach me from everything that had taken His place. My first lessons were to learn to love Him. He had only to reveal His Heart, and when I saw the depths of His Love for us all, and the wounds we are still giving Him, I could only surrender and love Him. The Lord asked me to lean on His Heart, just like John. When John leaned on His Heart, He had given Him the courage to be with Jesus below His Cross.

The Lord kept me hidden, teaching me and dictating to me for three years. I was alone. There was nobody to counsel me. Jesus explained to me the problems in the church. He also explained parts of Scriptures, for example, Apoc. 11:12,13,21,22.

Then exactly after these three years, the Lord pushed me to go out in public. I had no idea that the messages were Ecumenical, nor that they were imbued with the teachings of the Holy Spirit. I have received nine prophecies about Russia, where one of them came true.

The other big issue Jesus is bringing up is unity, and this is what I shall read to you today. I will take directly His words, which are printed and you have copies, I think. I will only take excerpts because the whole messages are very long.

This is one of His messages: "tell them that he who maintains to be just, yet remains divided, will eat from the fruit he has sown and will perish, tell them also how I abhor insincere hearts; their solemnities and their discourses weary me; tell them how I turn away from their loftiness and their rigidity; their judgment appears indeed great and impressive to men but not to Me, I cannot congratulate a dying church nearing putrefaction; tell those who want to hear that: <u>unless they lower their voices, they will never hear Mine</u>; should they lower their voices then they will begin to hear Mine and thus do My Will;" (NB 55, P 5)

"I am One, yet each one of them made a Christ of their own; I am the Head of My Body, yet all I see are <u>their</u> heads, not Mine; tell them to lower their heads <u>and they will see Mine;</u> tell

them to lower themselves so that I may be able to lift them to Me; ...tell everyone that I shall establish My Kingdom in the midst of <u>poverty</u>, those very ones who have time to hear My Spirit, adore Me and do My Will; in these My Soul rejoices! " (NB 55, P 6, 7)

"this fortress they have built to divide you is already condemned by Me; you are all brothers in Me, this is what you are to teach them to believe and persuade them to do; -- as for those who remain divided in body and spirit differentiating themselves under My Holy Name I tell them as I have told the church in Sardis; you are reputed to be alive in the eyes of the world, but not in your Maker's Eyes; revive what little you have left: it is dying fast and wherever the corpse is, there will the vultures gather;

unite!

assemble!

invoke My Name together!

consecrate My Body and My Blood together!

do not persecute the Way!

humble yourselves and bend to be able to unite and glorify Me; you speak of the Spirit but do not act in the Spirit; "you speak of the Way but you rank first to obstruct It! -- how little do you know Me... you call out My Name, yet you murder My children between the sanctuary and the altar; I tell you solemnly, all of this will be brought to you in the day of judgment; can you face Me and truly say: "I am reconciled with my brothers;" can you truly say: "I have not differentiated myself among brothers, under Your Holy Name; I have treated them as my equal;" when you present your case before Me I shall then say to your face: "away with you, you have not treated your brothers as your equal; you have massacred daily My Body; where is your triumph? while I was building, you were tearing down, <u>while I was reassembling you were scattering;</u> while I was uniting you were dividing!" yet, even today, if you come to Me as you are, I can heal you, I can transfigure you and you will glorify Me;" (NB 55, P 23-26)

"I am shouting and I am trying to break through your deafness to save you, and if I reproach you it is because of the Greatness of the Love I have for you; ...tell them that the Heart of the Lord is Love and that the Heart of the Law is based on Love; tell My people that I do not want administrators in My House, they will not be justified in My Day; because it is these very ones who have industrialized My House. I have sent you My Spirit to live in your hearts, this is why the Spirit that lives in you will show you that My Church will be rebuilt inside your hearts and you will acknowledge each other as your brother in your heart;" (NB 55, P 27-29)

And Jesus, asks, "will I, brother, one more season go through the pain I have been going through year after year? or will you give Me rest this time? am I going to drink one more season the cup of your division? or will you rest My Body and unify, for My Sake, the Feast of Easter?" in unifying the date of Easter, you will alleviate My pain, brother, and you will rejoice in Me and I in you; and I will have the sight of many restored;" (NB 55, P 30)

"I solemnly tell you: summon, assemble all of you, and listen this time to your Shepherd: I will lead you in the way that you must go; send My Message to the ends of the earth." (NB 55, P 32)

"Righteousness always preceded Me and Peace followed My Footsteps; am I to say the same for you? who will make up for the years of your division? solemnities and discourses do not interest Me; pretense and lip-service do not deceive Me either; oh daughter, what I wish them to understand, especially those who live in My Wounds is that My sorrow is great, and the reason why I have put some things rather strongly, is to enable them to preach something of the Spirit and not of the letter; I want to fill their Spirit with My Transcendent Light so that they see things with My Eyes and not with theirs; to see things with My Divine Light and not theirs; I am known to be Faithful and Righteous and it does not mean because they lack fidelity and righteousness, I too will show

them less Fidelity, Righteousness and Peace, and not come to rescue them; --- even if all of them turn away from Me and from My Ways, I will remain Faithful and True; " (NB 55, P 61-63)

"My Spirit will be at work restoring Peace among brothers and through My Cross and My Wounds I will unite you all in one single Body and have you glorify Me around

One Single Tabernacle

and the barrier which keeps you apart will be broken; the ban will be lifted and My Sacrificial Throne will be in its place. come to Me as little children that I may open the eyes of your soul that you may

see what Hope My Call holds for you."

(NB 55, P 63-64)

"---tell Me, are you not all alike, made by My Own Hands? who has not been made according to the likeness of My Image? because of man's base pride, My Father's Cup is filled with His Justice, because of their rigidity they are left uninhabited! many of them talk of unity and brotherhood, but their words are fallacious, void; -

prove yourselves in your Maker's Eyes by bending;
prove yourselves in your Maker's Eyes by unifying the date of Easter;
prove yourselves to Me by breaking bread together;
robe yourselves in majesty and splendor with humility and not with an outward appearance of religion and piety;
repent!

-- once you lived in humility simplicity and unbounded love with rich food covering your table; yes, the greatness of My Church exceeded everything and every living creature, because the Eucharist made the life of My Church; -- if My Church today lacks brightness it is because many of My churches have abolished My Perpetual Sacrifice; -- can one peer through this shadowed darkness and still claim they can see? can one boast of having escaped ambushes in this darkness? but so long as you say: "we see;" your guilt remains! I have said that there are other sheep I have that are not of the one fold and that I have to lead as well; but no sooner do I bring a wandering lamb back to the fold to lead a True Life in Me, no sooner do I restore his sight than you charge on him to take away the Kingdom of Heaven from him; -- could a devil open the eyes of the blind? could he make him cry out 'Abba!' so, unless you repent, My Father's Hand will fall upon you;" (NB 56, P 44-47)

"and now I make a special appeal to all those who are under My Name and are working for Unity and Peace; I ask you to come to Me like a child and face Me answering Me these questions: brothers, have you done everything you can to preserve the unity of My Body? tell Me brothers, where is the Peace I bequeathed to you, the Gift I have given you? Why are you continuously differentiating yourselves in Me? are you <u>sincerely</u> trying to be united again in your belief and practice? I tell you solemnly to <u>renew</u> your mind with a <u>spiritual</u> revolution, <u>a revolution of love;</u> forgive the grudges you have against each other and come to Me renewed, come to Me pure; wake up from your sleep! I am at your very doors knocking; do not be like salt which has lost its flavour, be like a tree putting out graceful shoots and bear the fruits of holiness, fulfill My Law by uniting and helping each other. like yesterday, I lift My Eyes to the Father and pray to Him: 'Holy Father, keep those You have given Me true to Your Name so that they may be one like Us', may they all be one. Father, Righteous One, remind them of My docility, My humility, My sincerity and My great love, so that they may end My Agony, this Agony which is the cause of so much bleeding in My Body, let them recognize their errors and reconcile so that when they come to receive Me by drinking Me and eating Me, they come worthily; Father, call the shepherds, and teach them to be yielding and docile towards each other, self-effacing and humble, may they realize My Atonement (this time of Lent) and seek true Wisdom in Me, amen. happy the man who listens to Me, happy those who follow My Ways, happy the man who humbles himself, happy the poor in spirit theirs is the kingdom of Heaven;

I, your Lord,
bless you and your families,
leaving My Sigh of Love on your forehead
and My Peace in your little hearts
and never forget that
Love is always with you;"

(NB 41, P 34-38)

Introduction

Fr. Henry Bordeaux, O.C.D.

Marylake Monastery, Little Rock, Arkansas

"Tell them that the Heart of their Lord is Love."
(NB 55, P 29)

With gratitude to the Holy and Triune God, I write this introduction to the messages of Jesus to Vassula and the world. Jesus wants them published because of their urgency.

I was a spiritual director for pilgrims to Medjugorje in May, 1990, when I met Fr. James Fannan, Vassula's spiritual director, who told me about the messages of Jesus to Vassula. I felt a deep attraction to, and interest in, these messages. Father said I could purchase them from a Medjugorje Peace Center. In August, I received the Messages of Peace and Love. I was awed at the profundity of Jesus' Love. Only the Scriptures taught me so much about the immensity of Jesus' Love and Mercy.

The messages are now a regular part of my daily reading. In December I received a powerful sign which authenticated the supernatural origin of these messages for me.

And now let us look at Jesus' instructions to Vassula and us. The messages unfold God's plans for the Church and the world. Hence, these new notebooks further develop the same themes expressed earlier by the Lord.

Perhaps we could begin with the fundamental reality underlying all of the messages which is Jesus' love, *"Tell them that the heart of their Lord is Love."* (NB 55, P 29)

These latest messages of Jesus to Vassula are the painful cries of the Lord Jesus: *"Fear Me and praise Me because the time has come for Me to sit in judgement." "The time of Mercy is running short; the time of My Reign on earth is close at hand." "My Kingdom will come suddenly upon you."* (NB 54, P 12, 13, 14)

The solemn description of the great illumination of the consciences of all men by God (NB 54, P 4) corresponds to a similar prophesy given in Garabandal.

The teaching of the Gospels on the absolute suddenness of the events which are to come is found here. (NB 54, P 14)

The day which Jesus calls *"My Day"* consists of the great purification and the outpouring of the Holy Spirit over the whole world in just as powerful a degree as it was in the early Church. The purification and the coming of the Holy Spirit is already happening. It will reach a much greater intensity.

Concerning the purification (and chastisement) Jesus says: *"I am telling you this that you may rejoice, because I too rejoice for this Day when Satan's head will be crushed by my Mother's heel."* (NB 54, P 18)

Also, *"There will still be a Fire before My Day, so do not fear or be sad, because without this Fire, the world's face cannot change."* (NB 54, P 19) Jesus is quite open with us: *"I am the Truth, and the Truth will always open His Heart and expose to you His fervent Plans as they are."* (NB 54, P 19-20) Concerning His Holy Spirit's coming, Jesus says: *"If you love Me, you would be glad to know that My Holy Spirit will come upon you in all His Force and in all His Glory."* (NB 54, P 24)

The days we are going through are those preceding the great purification. It is very near, nearer than we realize. Jesus says, *"The hour has come when constancy and faith, prayer and sacrifice are vital, they have become an urgency!"* (NB 54, P 31) He gives us a sublime prayer for these days preceding The Great Purification. (NB 54, P 31-36) *"The Holy One is tormented about that which has to come, saddened beyond description; I will* have to let *My Hand fall on this evil generation."* (NB 55, P 2) These words of Jesus describe the anguish of His Heart better than we can about what He calls the *"great distress."*

Jesus' desire for unity among us who believe in Him leaps up to us from these pages. It instructs us to bend our hearts, spirits, souls, and attitudes. He teaches all of us, Orthodox, Protestants, and Catholics to bend. We can be stiff-necked in our ideas of unity.

"For the sake of My Holy Name and the sake of My Love, unify My Churches; the real Christian is the one who is inwardly a Christian, and the real Unity is and will be IN the heart; unity will not be of the letter but of the Spirit." (NB 55, P 15-16)

Vassula's role in the unification of the Churches (the unification of the hearts of Christians) is important. *"Your mission, little one, is to bring My People under one Name, My Name, and break bread together. There is no need to worry; do your best and I will do the rest."* (NB 55, P 20-21)

The Lord is at work right now: *"The earth now is pregnant and in labor, My child, crying aloud in the pangs of childbirth; but the time of waiting is very soon over; I am already breathing on you, creation, reviving you, one after the other, purifying you all."* (NB 55, P 45-46)

The urgency to be poor in spirit is proclaimed by Jesus: *"How hard it is for those who have accumulated riches in their spirit to penetrate into My light."* (NB 56, P 4) *"They renounced My Spirit and allowed themselves to be guided by their own spirit."* (NB 56, P 6)

It is difficult, at times, to discern some of the prophecies of Jesus, but He, the Teacher, gives us direction. He invites us to come to Him, learn the immensity of His Love, receive His Love, and respond in love to Him by repenting and faithfully clinging to Him, obeying His Will. It is the age-old theme of the Father eagerly awaiting us, His daughters, His sons, to return. The greatest pain in the Heart of Our Lord Who Is Love is our lack of response. The

underlying truth of the messages, the reason for His plan of salvation for us, His urgent calling out to us is: *"Come, receive My Love, and be converted."*

Another firm truth: The Lord's Hour of Justice is just around the corner. He gives us hope as He tells us what the Holy Spirit will do in us. *"Once My Holy Spirit besieges you, you will all be transfigured."* (NB 56, P 40)

Jesus stresses the eternal union of His Heart with that of His Most Blessed Mother. *"Our Two Hearts are anointed and are living."* (NB 56, P 64) He identifies the Two Sacred Hearts as the two witnesses, the two olive trees, and the two lampstands of Apocalypse. Rev.11:1-8. These two lampstands are rejected by most: *"Our Two Hearts have become a plague to the people of the world."* But, *"Our Two Hearts you have combated shall prevail in the end."* (NB 57, P 1) We think immediately of Our Lady of Fatima's prophecy: In the end, My Immaculate Heart will triumph.

Concerning false locutions and prophecies, Jesus says: *"Be on your guard; many claim they hear Me, . . . but they are not mine. They do not consult Me."* (NB 57, P 13)

The Passive Night of the Soul, according to St. John of the Cross, is superbly described by Jesus in (NB 57, P 15-20) *"Although your soul will leap like on fire every time I will lift my hand to shatter all that keeps you captive; do not fear, do not run away in horror, allow Me to uproot in your soul all these infirmities."*

The prayer for this invasion of Jesus into the soul to completely purify it is found in NB 57, pp 25-30. It's profundity leaves us awed! May Jesus give to each reader of these lines the Holy Grace to be docile to the Plans of His Heart. Give us, O Father, most Gracious, a powerful Breath of Your Spirit to revive us all for Your Glory. Amen.

Prayers Given to Vassula

Jesus to Vassula
January 29, 1990

Lord, my God
Lift up my soul from this darkness into Your Light.
Envelop my soul into Your Sacred Heart.
Feed my soul with Your Word.
Annoint my soul with Your Holy Name.
Make my soul ready to hear Your Discourse.
Breath Your Sweet Fragrance on my soul, reviving it.
Ravish my soul to delight Your Soul.
Father, embellish me, Your Child,
by distilling Your Pure Myrrh upon me.

Your Spirit has given me life, and You who are the
Living Bread has restored my life.
You have offered me to drink Your Blood to be able to
share eternity with You in Your Kingdom,
and live with You for ever and ever.

Glory be to the Highest.
Glory be to the Holy of Holies.
Praised be Our Lord.
Praised be Our Lord, for His Mercy and His Love
reaches from age to age, and for ever will. Amen.

Mary to Vassula
May 15, 1990

Father, all merciful,
let those who hear and hear again,
but never understand,
hear Your Voice this time,
and understand that it is You,
the Holy of Holies.
Open the eyes of those who see but never perceive,
to see with their eyes this time
Your Holy Face and Your Glory.

Place Your Finger on their heart
so that their heart may open
and understand Your Faithfulness.

I pray and I ask all these things,
Righteous Father,
so that all the nation be converted and healed
through the wounds of
Your Beloved Son, Jesus Christ,
Amen.

Prayers Jesus Recommended to Vassula
(to be said daily)

Novena of Confidence to the Sacred Heart

O Lord, Jesus Christ,
to Your Most Sacred Heart I confide
this intention (state your request).

Only look upon me,
then do what Your Heart inspires,
Let Your Sacred Heart decide,
I count on It, I trust in It,
I throw myself on It's Mercy.

Lord Jesus, You will not fail me.
Sacred Heart of Jesus, I trust in Thee.
Sacred Heart of Jesus, I believe in
Thy love for me.
Sacred Heart of Jesus,
Thy Kingdom come.

O Sacred Heart of Jesus,
I have asked for many favors,
but I earnestly implore this one.

Take it. Place it in Thy Sacred Heart.
When the Eternal Father sees it
covered with Thy Precious Blood,
He will not refuse it.
It will be no longer my prayer,
but Thine, O Jesus.

O Sacred Heart of Jesus,
I place my trust in Thee.
Let me never be confounded.
Amen.

Prayer to St. Michael

St. Michael, the archangel, defend
us in the day of battle; be our
safeguard against the wickedness
and snares of the devil.

May God rebuke him, we humbly
pray, and do thou, O prince of the
heavenly host, by the power of

God, cast into hell, Satan,
and all the other evil spirits,
who prowl through the world
seeking the ruin of souls. Amen.

The Memorare of St. Bernard

Remember, O most gracious
Virgin Mary, that never was it
known that anyone who fled to
your protection, implored your
help, or sought your intercession,
was left unaided.
Inspired with this confidence, I fly
unto you. O Virgin of Virgins, my
Mother! To you I come, before you
I stand sinful and sorrowful.
O Mother of the Word Incarnate,
despise not my petitions, but in
your mercy, hear and answer me.
Amen.

lean on Me; blessed of My Soul, I give you My Peace; write:

"O Jerusalem*! turn your eyes to the east and to the west; turn your eyes to the north and to the south and I Am there! I tell you truly that once more My Spirit will be poured on you and My Image will be spread across the face of the world; what I have planned shall happen and what I have told you shall be fulfilled; come close

* That is: O generation!

to Me and listen carefully: today I come all the way to your doorstep holding the banner of Peace; I am coming to save you Jerusalem, on it is written: <u>Faithful and True</u>*¹, the <u>King of kings and the Lord of lords</u>*²; will I hear from you Jerusalem: "My King, it is You that I have to worship," or will you still be unaware of He who offers you His Peace.... now? will you in these last days before the Day of Retribution recognize My Holy Spirit who descended from above in all His Glory to

*¹ Ap. 19:11
*² Ap. 19:16

make house with you? during your whole lifetime, generation, you flouted My Law and turned away, rebelling; are you ever going to be prepared to meet Me, your God? I am soon going to pass through your City*! and it will be sooner than you think! these will be My last warnings; I solemnly tell you:

        wake up from your deep sleep!
        you are heading for your ruin,
        shake off the dust that covers you
        and rise from the dead,

* That is, through <u>us</u>. We are cities.

The End of Times*¹
        is nearer than you think;

1) soon, very soon, I shall suddenly open My Sanctuary in Heaven and there, your eyes unveiled, you will perceive, like a secret revelation: myriads of Angels, Thrones, Dominations, Sovereignties Powers, all prostrated around

        The Ark of the Covenant;

then, a Breath will slide over your face, and the Powers of Heaven will shake, flashes of lightning will be followed by peals of thun-

* The End of Times is NOT the End of the world, it is the end of an epoch.

5

der; "suddenly upon you will come a time of great distress, unparalleled since nations first came to existence;* for I will allow your soul to perceive all the events of your life-time; I will unfold them one after the other; to the great dismay of your soul, you will realize how much innocent blood your sins shed, from victim souls; I will then make your soul aware to see how you had never been following My Law; like an unrolled scroll, I will open The Ark of The Covenant

* Dn. 12:1

6

and make you conscious of your lawlessness; 2) if you would still be alive and standing on your feet, the eyes of your soul will behold a dazzling Light, like the glitter of many precious stones; like the sparks of crystal-clear diamonds, a Light so pure and so bright that although myriads of angels would be standing nearby, in Silence, you will not see them completely, because this Light will be covering them like a silverish golden dust, your soul will only perceive their form, not their face; then, in the midst of this dazzling Light,

7

your soul will see what they had once seen in that fraction of a second, that very moment of your creation....

they will see: He who held
you first in His Hands; The Eyes
that saw you first;
they will see: The Hands of
He who shaped you and
blessed you .... they will see:
The Most Tender Father, your Creator
all clothed in fearful splendour,
the First and the Last,

8

He who is, who was, and
is to come,
The Almighty,
The Alpha and the Omega:
The Ruler;

shrivelled with your awakening, your eyes will be transfixed in Mine which will be like two Flames of Fire.* ♡ your heart then will look back on its sins and will be seized with remorse; you will, in great distress and agony, suffer your lawlessness, realizing how you were constantly profaning My Holy Name and how

* Ap. 19:12

9

you were rejecting Me, your Father .... panic-stricken, you will tremble and shudder when you will see yourself as a decaying corpse, devastated by worm and by vulture; and if your legs will still be holding you up, I will show you what your soul, My Temple and My Dwelling was nursing, all the years of your life; instead of My Perpetual Sacrifice you will see to your dismay, that you were fondling The Viper and that you had erected this Disastrous Abomination of which the prophet Daniel spoke, in the most profound domain of

10

your soul;

The Blasphemy;

The Blasphemy, that cut off all your heavenly bonds linking you to Me and making a gulf between you and Me, your God; — when this Day comes, the scales of your eyes will fall, so that you may perceive how naked you are and how within you, you are a land of drought .... unhappy creature, your rebellion and your denial of The Most Holy Trinity turned you into a renegade and a persecutor of My Word; — your laments and your

11

waiting will be heard only by you then; I tell you : you will mourn and you will weep, but your laments will only be heard by your own ears; — I can only judge as I am told to judge and My judging will be just; as it was in Noah's time, so will it be when I will open the Heavens and show you The Ark of the Covenant; " for in those days before the Flood, people were eating, drinking, taking wives, taking husbands, right up to the day Noah went into the ark, and they suspected nothing till the Flood came

12

and swept all away"; * this is how it will be in this Day too; and I tell you, if that time had not been shortened by the intercession of your Holy Mother, the martyr saints and the pool of blood shed on earth, from Abel the Holy to the blood of all My prophets, not one of you would have survived !

I, your God, am sending angel after angel to announce that My Time of Mercy is running short and that the Time of My Reign on earth is close at hand; I am sending

* Mt. 24 : 38 - 39

13

My angels to witness of My Love" to all who live on earth, every nation, race, language and tribe."*¹ I am sending them out as apostles of the last days to announce that : "the Kingdom of the world would become like My Kingdom of above and that My Spirit will reign for ever and ever "*² in your midst; I am sending My servants the prophets to cry out in this wilderness that you should :

"Fear Me and praise Me

because the Time has come

*¹ Ap. 14:6
*² Ap. 11:15

14

for Me to sit in

judgment ! "*

My Kingdom will come suddenly upon you, this is why you <u>must</u> have constancy and faith till the end; —

— My child, pray for the sinner who is unaware of his decay;

pray and ask the Father to forgive the crimes the world ceaselessly commits;

pray for the conversion of souls,

pray for Peace ♡

ΙΧΘΥΣ

* Ap 14:7

15

19.9.91

My Lord, You are my cup and my very soul rejoices in You. Your great Tenderness upholds me to cross this desert, my side by Your Side, my hand in Your Hand. —"It is for You I am putting up with insults that cover me with shame, and make me a stranger to my own brothers, an alien to my country's other sons; but zeal for Your House devours me!" Ps. 69:7-9

Nassula, let Me whisper My Words in your ear, that you may glorify Me; — do not listen, My lamb, to what the world says, because from it comes nothing good, listen to Me, I who am your Father, and by listening carefully, you will carry out the work I have confided you with; trust Me, My child, and

16

come to Me for advice, come to Me for consolation; come to Me when the fever of this world rises against you and burns you, come quickly to Me, your Abba, and I will heal your blisters; I am He who loves you most tenderly and I will nurse you always back to health; I shall always soothe the wounds the world inflicts on you for the sake of My Holy Name and for witnessing on My Love; remember: up in Heaven I Am watches over you and takes care of all your problems; remember too that everything you do is not for your

17

interests nor for your glory, but for the Interests and the Glory of He who sent you;
♡ let My Spirit of Truth shine on you so
that you, in your turn, reflect My Image,
reminding the world of My True Face, since
the world seems to have forgotten My True
Image; — in a short time all of you will
learn how to live a

<u>True Life in God</u>

and be one with Me as the Holy Trinity is
One and the same, because all Three of Us
agree ♡ — My little children, I shall not be

18

long, I am already on My Way of Return; I
am telling you this before it happens, because
when it does happen, you may believe that
this Voice you have been hearing all these
years, came from Me; I am telling you this so
that you may rejoice, because I too, rejoice
for this Day when Satan's head will be
crushed by My Mother's heel; — hear Me:
I shall pour out My Spirit on this evil
generation to entice hearts and lead everyone
back to the complete Truth, to live

<u>a Perfect Life in Me your God;</u>

19

but be brave, because there will still be a
Fire before My Day, so do not fear nor be
sad, because without this Fire, the world's
face cannot change .... and when it comes, it
will show the world how wrong it was; it will
show its godlessness; its rationalism, materialism,
selfishness, pride, greed and its wickedness, in
short, all those vices the world worships;
    no one can say that I have not been telling
you the outset of My Plans; no one can say
that I have been hiding My Plans from you;
        I am The Truth

20

and The Truth will always open His Heart and
expose to you His fervent Plans <u>as they are</u> ....
the Truth will always give you the Choice of
proving yourselves to Him; — if I had not
spoken to you, if I had not been opening <u>now</u>
the Heavens to you, you would be excused, but
I <u>have</u> been calling you day and night, without ceasing I <u>have</u> been sending you My angels
to speak to you; I raised from nothing, wretched
souls and formed them into fervent disciples to
go and knock on your doors and repeat to you
the Words I Myself have given them; no,

21

they were not speaking as from themselves, but were only repeating the Knowledge that I Myself have instructed them with ♡ they went to you in their poverty and barefoot to tell you of the things that are to come, not adding nor deducting anything from that which I have given them; all they said was taken from Wisdom Herself; — now, I solemnly tell you, that when that Day of Purification comes, many will be sorrowful to the point of death for not having allowed My Holy Spirit of Truth to enter their house,* but have welcomed in His place

* that is: their soul.

22

the Viper, the Abomination of the desolation, and shared their meal side by side with My enemy; they welcomed inside their house the one who apes the Holy One, they worshipped the Deceiver, who taught them to misconceive My Holy Spirit:

My Holy Spirit, the Giver of Life and
The Inner Power of their soul

He who breathed an active soul into them and inspired a living spirit ♡ — I tell you solemnly, My Fire will descend in this world quicker than you expect it to come, so that those without sight of their sins may suddenly

23

see their guilt; it is in My Power to bring this day forward and it is again within My Power to shorten this Hour, for this Hour will bring so much distress that many would curse the hour of their birth, they would want the valleys to open and swallow them, the mountains to fall on them and cover them, the vulture to devastate them quickly, they would want to dash themselves to pieces; but no one will escape from this Hour; those that truly love Me will suffer only for not having done more for Me; they too will be cleansed; but

24

woe to those who rejected Me and refused to recognize Me, they have their judge already; the Truth that was given to them will be their judge on that Day; — you heard Me say many times from My mouthpieces that
" the Day of the Lord is at hand "
and that My Return is imminent; if you love Me you would be glad to know that My Holy Spirit will come upon you in all His force and in all His glory; if you love Me you will continue to pray for the conversion of all My children who are unaware and still live

25

under Satan's power; if anyone loves Me as
I love you all, he will listen to Me and will remain faithful up to the end of his ministry;
My little children, if you loved Me, you would
perform even greater works than those I performed while on earth, but no one has performed
anything greater yet because of the so little
faith you have in Me, and the ever so little
love you have for one another; no one yet
has loved Me as much as I love you; but on
the Day of Purification you will understand
how little you have done because I will show

26

My Holy Face in you; — you hear those
Footsteps? they are Mine; you hear the sound
of My Breath already? it is the sweet sound
of My Holy Spirit blowing through your wilderness and your aridity; you felt a Breath
slide over your face? do not fear; like the Dove's
wings, My Holy Spirit touched you slightly while
hovering above you ♡ O come! come to Me
and as Moses lifted up the serpent in the desert,
I too will lift your soul up to Me and revive
you! as I was lifted up in Heaven you too
will be lifted up to Me to be nursed on My

27

Breast; O come to Me! get thirsty again, thirst
for My Everlasting Wells, thirst to be with Me,
your God! I will without hesitation offer you
to drink and turn My Water into a spring inside
you, welling up to eternal life, for from My
Breast flow fountains of living water, an inexhaustible Source; O come to Me! hunger again
for My Bread, and you will not die! today,
as yesterday, I stand up and cry out:
    "if any man is thirsty, let him come
to Me! let the man come and drink who
believes in Me!"* My forbearance is great,

    * (Jn. 7: 37)

28

and although I know you are sinners and you
have polluted the earth with innocent blood,* if
you come to Me repentant, I will forgive your
guilt and your crime; I am an Abyss of
Grace; do not be afraid .... do not fear Me,
fear rather the Hour if it finds you unaware
and asleep; — this is the Voice of your Father;
this is the Voice of the Sublime Source of
Love; this is the Voice of He who once said:
        "Let there be light!"
and there was light; come to Me and I

* There was a stress, that Jesus put in my mind, on
abortions.

29

shall give you My Spirit without reserve;

do not be like the soldiers who shared out My clothing and cast lots for them at the foot of My Cross; come to Me with John's spirit, <u>come to Me out of love</u>; come to Me to console Me and be with Me; — the Hour is coming, when the world will find itself only in distress and darkness, the black-ness of anguish and will see nothing but night; bewildered, they will call out to Me, but I shall not reply, I shall not listen to their cry; frenzied, they will blaspheme

30

My Revelation, Wisdom and the Truth; the whole world will be inundated by distress upon seeing the

Ark of the Covenant,

My Law;

many will fall and be broken, rocked and shaken because of their lawlessness; — when the heavens will tear open, like a curtain ripped in half, showing them how they flung My Glory for a worthless imitation*, like stars that fall from heaven they shall fall, reali-zing then how Folly led them astray; how

* Allusion to Dn. 8: 11-12: That is : The Holy Communion

31

by trying to climb up to the summit and rival Me was only folly! when that Day comes, I will show the world how wicked it was, how they befriended the Rebel and dialogued with him rather than with the Holy One; the hour has come when constancy and faith, prayer and sacrifice are vital, they have become an URGENCY!

My little children, you who are sad now will rejoice later on; come let us pray:

Father all Merciful

raise me up to Your Breast,

32

allow me to drink from the

Running Streams of Eternal Life,

and by this I shall know that

I enjoy Your favour,

O come and rescue me, before

the Hour comes upon me;

cure me,

for I have sinned against You ♡;

Father,

Your Lips are moist with Grace,

Your Heart is a blazing Furnace of Love,

Your Eyes are Two Flames of consuming Fire,

33

O Father,
Your Beauty is Perfection in itself,
Your Majesty and Splendour leave even the
brightest of Your angels dazzled,
Wealthy in Virtue and Grace,
do not hide Your Holy Face from
me, when the Hour comes;
come and anoint me with the oil of love,
God, hear my prayer,
listen to my supplicating voice!
I must fulfil the vows I made You;
Eternal Father,

34

although the current is opposing me,
I trust,
I know,
I believe,
that Your Arm will be there,
to lift me and pull me out of this current;
O how I long to gaze on
Your Sanctuary and see Your Glory
in the Ark of the Covenant!
O how my soul languishes to gaze
on the Rider of the Heavens
who carries the Name:

35

Faithful and True,
He who will sweep away iniquity
from the world,
He who is Just;
O come and cover me with Your Cloak
since Your Love is known for its generosity,
O Father! do not brush me off
like I deserve because of my sins,
but help me, provide me with my
Daily Bread,
and keep me safe and away
from the Viper's fangs;

36

make me heiress of Your House,
make me Your child of Light,
make me a perfect copy of the
Supreme Martyr, to glorify You,
for ever and ever; ♡
amen ♡

Heaven belongs to you My child;* live for Me,
breathe for Me, have Me as First, love Me, My
child and all that I have is yours; by your
love and your faithfulness My House will be your

* After having read the prayer God had dictated to me for
Him, He was very touched and with emotion in His
Voice told me what followed.

37

house too; — rely on Me your Abba; come close to Me and take your place in My

Sacred Heart ♡

23.9.91

All day long, I sigh for You my Yahweh, my own,
Your love that You showed me I cannot forget.
— Never. — Your Kindness my Yahweh, my own,
I shall remember as long as I live.
I pine away with Love for You my Yahweh, day
after day, and I no longer wish to associate
myself in this world that wounds You, and to
know that I am among the first who wound You...
My soul wants to proclaim all Your wonders
to the world and my feet want to run to
the hill-tops and cry out to the world:
"Your Creator is Your Husband!
His Name, Yahweh Sabaoth.
Yes, like a forsaken wife, distressed in
spirit, Yahweh calls you back. Does a
man cast off the wife of his youth? says your God."
Is. 54:5-6

38

Yet I fear, O my Yahweh, my Abba and my own.
My soul yearns and pines away for Your
House and
all I long for now is to be with You.
So do not ask me why my
spirit is downcast,
since my sighs are no secret for You and all
that I sigh for is known to You:
my soul awaits You, my Yahweh,
come and invade me,
come and consume me.

Vassula.... do not hide My child* .... daughter
of Egypt, I have appointed you as assayer of
many nations and you are very precious to

* I was hoping that I need no longer go out to the
nations and be present witnessing. I was hoping that
my Father consents with my desires : to stay
home, meditate, love Him, meet Him in writing,
meet Jesus in the Holy Eucharist and thus avoid crowds.

39

Me; do not misunderstand Me, I do not need
you and you are not indispensible for this
work either; but having chosen you, a nothing,
glorifies Me, and purifies you; then, everything
I own I wish to share with you; do not
fear proclaiming My Messages, My Holy Spirit
will fill you with My Words and you will
boldly proclaim My Word ♡ so go now to
those to whom I send you, I shall not abandon you, nor will I leave you uninhabited,
My Holy Spirit is your Guide and your
Counsellor; I have only begun to reap My

40

Harvest..... reap with Me .... you have not sown
this Harvest; I did all the sowing in you
and now I want it everywhere; now that the
Harvest is ready all I ask from you is to reap
it with Me, My daughter; offer your assistance
as a sacrifice; I am not asking you much ....
.... what do you see, daughter?

Your Son's Holy Face, smothered from pain; His
Face is like on the Holy Shroud.

is this not enough a reason for proceeding
and sacrificing a little bit of your time
and energy? look again, daughter ....

41

what do you see now, Nassula?

I see something like a soft <u>red</u> cloud filling the sky, hovering above us and yet moving like mist and taking more of the sky; it moves gently but steadily.

write: " like dawn there spreads across the mountains a vast and mighty host, such as has never been before, such as will never be again to the remotest ages ;" (Joël 2:2) yes, it is near .... and now what do you see, Nassula?

  Live human torches.

see carefully those very souls I created .... these

42

shall never reach the Room I had prepared for them, these souls are under Satan's power, and they will not share My Kingdom nor My Glory; they are heading for their damnation .... tell Me, have I deprived any soul of My Love, My Glory and My Kingdom?

  — No, Lord. but they have chosen not to love Me and willingly followed Satan; they cut off, by their own free will, the bonds of our union; and now look again, Nassula, what do you see?   O Lord, a Woman, sitting on a white rock, I see Her from the back, She's

43

wearing a long black dress and has Her Head also covered with a long black scarf. She appears to be in great distress and is doubled with Her pain. — I see myself approach Her, She lifts Her Face, and I start to weep too with Her. It's Jesus' Mother, our Mother, Her Face is very pale and filled with tears. Upon seeing me She stretched Her left Hand and pressed it on my arm.

I am the Woman of Sorrows, familiar with misery, I am the one who will recover for you: <u>Hope</u>; I am the one who will crush and trample with My heel the serpent's head; My Eyes weep ceaselessly these days without relief, My Eyes have grown sore over all My children; Nassula, My daughter, do not close your ear to God,

44

do not close your ear to My request; you heard Me weeping, I have defended your cause, and always will; when the Lord fastens you to Him, it is out of Love to pour out His Heart in your heart; today,* <u>to you in turn His Cup will be passed</u>, do not refuse to drink, hesitant you must not be; your streets are polluted with innocent blood, and Our Hearts are sick, this is the reason for My Tears, this is the reason why the Lord will share His Cup with you; <u>treason barricades unity among brothers, insincerity of heart induces God's Cup to augment</u>; they wrenched the Body

* meaning, these coming days.

45

of My Son, divided It, mutilated It and para-
lized It; I am reminding you all that through
Him, all of you have in the One Spirit your
way to come to the Father, yet you remain
divided under My Son's Name; you speak of
unity and peace and yet stretch a net for
those who practice it; God cannot be deceived
nor is He convinced by your arguments; the
Kingdom of God is not just words on the
lips, the Kingdom of God is love, peace, unity
and faith in the heart: it is the Lord's Church
united in One inside your heart; the Keys to

46

Unity are: Love and Humility; Jesus never
urged you to divide yourselves, this division
in His Church was no desire of His ♡ I implore
My children to unite in heart and voice and
rebuild My Son's primitive Church in their
heart; I am saying My Son's primitive
Church, since that Church was constructed on
Love, Simplicity, Humility and Faith; I do
not mean you to reconstruct a new edifice, I
mean you to reconstruct an edifice inside your
heart, I mean you to knock down the old
bricks inside your heart, bricks of disunion,

47

intolerance, unfaithfulness, unforgiveness, lack
of love, and reconstruct My Son's Church by
reconciling; you need intense poverty of the
spirit and an overflow of wealth of generosity,
and not until you understand that you will
have to bend, will you be able to unite ♡ —
so My Vassula, join Me in My prayer, as you
saw Me praying before; I am with you My
child, very much; comply with Love's desires,
Jesus will never abandon you, be united in
your love with Him, for one purpose:
to glorify Him ♡

48

now, daughter*, do you understand why you should
not give up reaping with Me? keep on praying;
and bless those who persecute you; your hour
has not yet come, My dove; I will be gentle
with you and you will be all the more loved
by Me; do not try to understand what is
beyond your power; drive in the sickle when
you see Me driving in My Sickle; do not delay
your step, follow in time with My Pace; if I
delay, delay too; speak up when I give you
the signal and keep silent when I look at

* The Father's Voice again came back.

49

you; always defend to death The Truth; scathed you shall be from time to time, but I shall allow it just enough to keep your soul pure and docile; know that I am always by your side; reap when I reap; learn to be patient as I am Patient; be very humble and effaced; I have entrusted you with My Interests* to work with Me at My side, and I have appointed others too to join their services in this work ♡ - Vassula, My child, a little longer, a very little and your soul will fly to Me, so

* I also heard: Ministry

50

there is no reason to feel downcast as you tell Me, you have but to lift your head and look Who comes all the way to your room, Who sups with you, Who shepherds you; ask Me to forgive yours sins, so that you may receive My Peace and that you may have joy, again; tell My children that soon I will send My Holy Spirit in full force to shepherd you and lead you all back into the true Fold and live a

<u>True Life in Me your God</u>

α ☧ Ω

51

26.9.91

My eyes are always on You, O my God. The close secret* to You is given to those who love You and fear You.

You have lifted my soul from the pit to discover Your Sacred Heart's Wealth,
I have discovered
the Mercy Your prophets spoke of,
I have discovered
the Love and Meekness Your disciples tasted,
I have discovered
the Peace You Yourself have given us.
In Your Sacred Heart, You allowed my soul
to discover
that Suffering is Divine
and Mortification agreeable in Your Eyes.

Then in my soul came a brilliant Light, and like a tuneful noise of doves, I heard and felt a Breath slide over my face and You filled me with Your Mysteries.

* meaning: the intimacy

52

Taste more of My Secrets, My child, by being obedient to My Law; lower even <u>more</u> now your voice so you may hear <u>only</u> Mine; lower your head, so that Mine would be seen; lower yourself so that I can lift you up to Me; many a time you inspect the Secrets of My Sacred Heart with your own light, you have only to ask Me, My child, and I will pour in your eyes My Transcendent Light and it will fill your entire soul; see to it then, My child, that the light inside you comes from Me; then, only then, My

53

priest, will you understand that My Works are Sublime, Glorious and Majestic; only then, pupil of Mine, will you understand as I desire you to understand why Humility allowed Himself to be disgraced, disfigured, despised and pierced and gave His Life as a ransom for many; — I have come to stir your love and rouse it, see? so do not shield your flesh from pain nor from any mortification; allow the Seal of your Saviour to be on your flesh as well as in your soul so that a complete transformation be done inside you,

54

EVERYTHING then that your nature repelled objected to and looked at with disdain, will appear to you Divine ♡

Grant Lord that everything You say, be done. — Lower my head, lower me and lower my voice! I do not want to appear empty handed in Your Presence; no, I do not want to end up in Your Presence with empty hands. And those human thoughts my nature finds natural, uproot them and burn each one of them.

devote your soul entirely to Me and reflect on My Law before it comes upon you; do not forget how your nature had reduced you to desert, and desolation; I shall rid your human thoughts if you allow Me and replace them

55

with My Thoughts to glorify Me; I will give you a courageous heart, My little one, to be able to face My opponents and resist their contradictions; I shall give you an eloquence of speech, an endurance and a resistance to the menaces of your persecutors who are My persecutors too; I shall give you courage to stand with confidence; you are My seed and because the Harvest is ready, and the crop ready to be reaped, I do not lose time as you have noticed; I reap without ceasing to feed many who are at the point of death;

56

so My beloved; "put your sickle in too and reap": harvest time has come and the harvest of the earth is ripe;* allow Me to widen the space of your heart, for now your Captor will fill you with His Knowledge and His Confidences, I am only waiting to be gracious to all of you and reveal to each one of you My Riches, My Generosity and My Love; I am telling you today all this so that My Word goes from this generation to the next; and you who are learning, will, in your turn teach your own children ♡ if they listen and do as I say,

* Ap. 14; 15

57

their days will end up in happiness; so
turn to Me and praise My Works; meditate
on My Wonders; ΙΧΘΥΣ ⟨><⟩

St Michael's Feast. 29. 9. 91

St. Michael:

I love you child of God; trust Me ♡

The Lord: rest in My Heart, I the Lord bless
you; come, My Heart is your nest
                                          ♡ 30. 9. 91

I give thanks to Your Name for Your Love and
Mercy; though I live in a place where I am surrounded by persecutors, false witnesses and abuses,
You keep me alive and on my feet. You fill
my table, and like a most tender mother You
feed me with Your own Hand. O Lord, pity
me, sometimes I have trouble more than I
could stand, and if I did not have You near

58

me, I would be finished! I want a complete
peace between brothers.

I say peace be with you! stand up and
call My servant*! I am the Lord of Peace
not of dissension and I have offered you My
Heart; let no one be deceived; those who linger
over grudges for too long, I shall withdraw
from them My Heart and all the favours I
so generously offered them; unless My servant
collaborates with love and stops brooding over
this sin, I tell you that I will withdraw all
of My favours: never model your conduct

* Message for someone.

59

on the One who divides; I am giving you a
Treasure of Unity, ever so frail; learn to
protect this Treasure
                         ♡   ☧
                                    30. 9. 91

Jesus?

I Am; little one, saturated by Me, you will
not fail Me; at your side I Am and always
will be; bless Me for those who never do;
reveal Me without fear, without doubt and
hell shall not prevail; caress Me, yes, look in
My Face and say: "Jesus I love You, You
are my life, my smile, my hope, my joy,
my everything; be blessed;" come, rest in My

60

Heart and allow Me to rest in yours ♡
                                          1. 10. 91

To the Canadian pilgrims (140 laymen and 9 priests),
at Lens, who came to spend a week with me.

tell them that today like yesterday and always
I bless them; let every ear open and hear,
every heart open to receive My Word:

      all I ask from them is love, fidelity
and a continuous prayer; I shall be with
you soon; come ♡
                                 (In the evening)
My Lord You have come and revived my soul
and since then a new life trickles in me, because
this Stream flows from Your Own Sanctuary.
- Look at Your child Lord? Alive again!
You have redeemed me, You have redressed

61

me and You showed me the fathoms of Your Love. Your fragrance mesmerized me and Your Beauty left me forever dazzled and hung on You. Your Tenderness and Graciousness set a spring in me; blessed be Your Name for ever and ever! in You every race shall be blessed and all nations will in the end one day, united in one, cry out:

'Blessings on him who comes in
the Name of the Lord!'

For as the rain allows the earth to sprout, so will the River* from Your Sanctuary irrigate Your cities.*²

To the Canadian pilgrims. 2.10.91

peace be with you; let this day be a day of joy! soon My salvation will come, so be prepared to receive Me; besides you whom I have already gathered under My Name, there are others

*¹ Holy Spirit   *² our souls

62

shall gather; ask My children to meditate on:

(Is. 54:5) 'For your Creator is your
husband, Yahweh Sabaoth is
His Name'

let everyone today call Me,
Spouse;

pray for the peace of the world, pray for Our intentions ♡   ΙΧΘΥΣ 🐟

3.10.91

During mass together with the Canadian pilgrims, Jesus said to me in a locution:

" I have sent you My friends."

63

4. 10. 91

For the Canadian pilgrims.

lean on Me, give Me all your worries, thrust them all in My Heart and I shall annihilate them; bless Me as I bless you, love Me as I love you; creation! realize that all I ask from you is a return of love! I confer on you everlasting blessings; so today and every day put your trust in Me; draw from My Heart's Wells and I shall fill you, investing you with My splendour; I know your hardships and your extreme poverty so do not be afraid to come to Me as you are;

64

— poverty infatuates Me —

welcome Me as I welcome you; — go in Peace and be the witnesses of Me who loves you more than any other man; be witnesses of Me who offered you His Sacred Heart ΙΧΘΥΣ 🐟

5. 10. 91

To the Canadian pilgrims.

peace be with you; restore My House; — I am sending you like lambs among wolves, but do not fear, I Am is with you; — embellish My House by your devotion to My Sacred Heart and the Immaculate Heart of your Mother ♡ I bless

1

you all, leaving the Sigh of My Love on your forehead IΧΘΥΣ ⟨⟩

7.10.91

I want to put everything I have for Your Glory. I do not have much, in fact I have next to nothing because I am insufficient, poor, weak and most wretched, yet whatever I might have, take it my Lord.

My closeness* to you has lit a fire inside you and saved you and others; — I want your free will, offer yourself to Me and I shall make rivers flow out of you. I need intense poverty to bring My Works out on the surface; I will supply your soul since you are My bride; Vassula, your cities are filled with dead and their stench

* His intimacy.

2

rises all the way to heaven; they are decomposing by the millions, pray, pray for peace, love, faith and unity ♡ the Holy One is tormented about that which has to come, saddened beyond description; I will have to let My Hand fall on this evil generation; daughter, for My sake, take My Cross of Unity and carry It across the world; go from country to country and tell those who speak of unity, yet never cease to think the contrary and continue to live the contrary that <u>their division has separated My Heart from theirs</u>; shout and eventually My

3

Voice shall break through their deafness; I am with you in this desolation so do not fear ♡ I have entrusted you with My Cross; this Cross will sanctify you and save you, and so carry It with love and humility; invoke My Name without cease; your Mission, My child, is to witness for love and to demonstrate My Holiness in their lack of love and fidelity, go forward without fear and be My Echo ♡ witness with joy, with fervour, witness with love for Love ♡ whenever My enemies pierce you, <u>rejoice</u>! and offer all your wounds to

4

Me and I shall soothe you immediately; everytime you lift your eyes looking for Me, My Heart rich in Mercy will not resist you; you are My child whom I adopted, raised and fed, so do not fear men, they cannot destroy you; soon I shall set you free; in the meantime go around with My Cross of Unity and glorify Me, be the

<u>defender</u>

of the Truth and of the One Church I Myself had established; go to every nation and present yourself to them ♡ tell them that I

5

want Peace and One Church under My Holy Name; tell them that he who maintains to be just, yet remains divided, will eat from the fruit he has sown and will perish ♡ tell them also how I abhor insincere hearts; their solemnities and their discourses weary Me, tell them how I turn away from their loftiness and their rigidity; their judgement appears indeed great and impressive to men but not to Me, I cannot congratulate a dying church nearing putrefaction; tell those who want to hear that:

6

unless they lower their voices,
they will never hear Mine;
should they lower their voices then they will begin to hear Mine and thus do My Will; I am One, yet each one of them made a Christ of their own; I am The Head of My Body, yet all I see are their heads, not Mine; tell them to lower their heads and they will see Mine; tell them to lower themselves so that I may be able to lift them to Me; — do not let them terrify you, My child; be patient as I am patient; be prudent by

7

remaining by My side; you will wear My Jewels* so that you remain faithful to Me, they will keep reminding you of Me; pray, My bride, pray to your Spouse and I shall in the end reward you; glorify Me and I tell you: toil, sacrifice and nothing will go in vain ♡ tell everyone that I shall establish My ♡ Kingdom in the midst of
poverty,
those very ones who have time to hear My Spirit, adore Me and do My Will; in these My Soul rejoices! daughter, I

* His Cross, Nails and Thorned Crown.

8

love you in spite of your misery; allow Me to continue My Works in you; adjust to Me as I adjust to you and through you My Presence will be felt, and in you I shall draw this generation to unity; be confident because I am with you; My Seal is on your fore-head and with this Seal and with My Grace, My Kingdom on earth will be established as I want; have My Peace, remember: I am with you all the time; come, enter into My Wounds ΙΧΘΥΣ

9

13. 10. 91

There is no one, my Lord, in my heart but You. Little by little You correct me; You have won my heart showering blessing upon blessing on me.

But am I doing Your Will now? Am I near You following You? Am I coming to my neighbour's help as far as I can? Am I following Your Commandments? Am I enjoying Your favour still?

learn to lean on Me; - daughter, are you willing to continue carrying the Cross I have predestined for you?

I am willing, so long as I do not lose You and am with You, united and one.

do you know what this means and what it requires?

Sacrifice, abasement, humility, effacement, love, faith, hope, docility, self-abnegation, prayer, prayer,

10

prayer, patience, penance, mortification, suffering, fasting, and trust in You? and a spirit of forgiveness.

you have said well, but it is not just to know these things; you want to remain in My favour? then you must put everything you mentioned into practice ♡ the Kingdom of Heaven is like a trophy, he who wins it will cherish it; again, the Kingdom of Heaven will be given to those who come with their hands full of good fruit ♡ - and so My Vassula, I intend to rebuild My Church on the virtues you have mentioned; if you walk

11

with Me you will not be lost; do not be tempted to look to your left or to your right; as I had said to My disciples: 'salute no one on the road';* you want to serve Me as you say, you must follow Me then with your Cross of Peace, Love and Unity to glorify Me; do not look with consternation on the other crosses I lay on your way, since they all come from Me; glorify Me; your table is always full and your cup brimming over, so do not complain for nothing; I shall probe you and test your love for Me now and then to

* Lk. 10 : 4

12

build you spiritually ♡ do not drag your feet behind Me, follow ♡ My pace lightheartedly; rest in Me when you are weary and allow Me to rest in you when I feel weary; - listen now to your Holy One: do not be taken away by every wind that comes your way, be rooted in Me and you will not be uprooted, daughter; enrich My Church with all the Knowledge I have given you and tell them that the Heart of the Lord is an Abyss of Love, yet no man is fully aware of its depths nor of its riches; I know you are frail, daughter, yet

13

have you lacked resources? trust Me, trust Me,
and be the reflection of what Unity will be like;
do not be like those who persist in differentiating
themselves under My Holy Name; do not be
like those who pretend that Unity is appeal-
ing to them and remain dead to their word
achieving nothing but a resentment from the
Father; both the Father and I abhor their
arguments, contrary to what they think ♡
  yet nothing retains Me from crying out
to these men of power:
      " descend! descend from your thrones

14

and may these scales on your eyes fall to see
what a desolation you have made out of My
House! you have robbed My Sanctuary and
all that was within it! you shattered the
Shepherd's staff not only in half but in
splinters! but today, open your eyes and see!
  keep your eyes open and you will get to know
poverty, sackcloth and barefootedness, keep your
eyes open and with one look get to know My
Heart; " — I could utter only one word
in their assemblies and with that single word
unite My Church; but the glory of Heaven

15

will be given to Me by Poverty, Wretchedness
and by those they call contemptible; I will
have My House rebuilt by strangers, for in them
I will place a spirit of zeal, a spirit of fidelity;
then your stores will be filled again and
your vats overflowing with My new wine ♡
  if you say you love Me and call yourself under My Name, then for the sake of
My Holy Name and the sake of My Love:
          unify My churches;
the real Christian is the one who is inwardly
a Christian, and the real Unity is and will

16

be in the heart; Unity will not be of the
letter but of the spirit; —
if you love Me, daughter, as you say, embrace
the Cross I have given you; your feet then will
not stumble, nothing in this world is Its equal;
let your gaze never leave My Gaze; pupil?
come, follow Me ... ΙΧΘΥΣ 🐟
                                13. 10. 91

Vassula, I prayed for you to the Father; it is
I, Jesus; concentrate on what has been assigned
you; — now write: * peace be with you;
I heard you call Me: " Father! "

* Message for the prisoners

17

Here I Am;

do you wish to come back? I shall frown on
you no more since I am Infinite Mercy; I shall
not pronounce sentence on you either; your heart
is what I am seeking ♡ I need love; I am thirsty
for love; My Lips are parched for lack of love;
I have decided not to look on your past, only
at the present; the Queen of Heaven* is by My
side and of all women She, persistently, prayed
for you, more than all Sovereignties, Dominations,
Thrones, Powers and Angels; more than any
created thing; so welcome Her in your prayers,

* Our Lady.

18

honour Her as I honour Her; you are all bap-
tised in Me and there should not be any dis-
tinction between brothers; if you only knew
what I am offering you today you would not
hesitate to offer Me your heart and your aban-
donment; come back to Me and do not fear,
the One who speaks to you now is your Holy
Companion; He who loves you most; believe in
My Love, consider and meditate on My Passion;
offer Me your heart and I shall turn it into
a garden with the subtlest odours, where I,
your King, can take My rest ♡ allow Me

19

to make it My Property, and you shall live;
do not turn your heart away from Me, do not
keep Me at a distance, speak to Me freely; I
am listening; I invite you all to meditate on
these words:

- repay evil with love -
- imitate Me -

and remember, I am with you all the time;
never ever forget this; I bless each one of you,
leaving the Sign of My Love on your forehead

ΙΧΘΥΣ 〈⟩━○ Jesus Christ Beloved Son
of God and Saviour

20

14.10.91

Lord? I am; evangelize with love
for Love; be rooted in Me, My child; hand
over everything to Me and allow Me to be
your Spiritual Director, directing you and
giving you My directives for the unification
of My Churches; you are to be a sign for them
and they will learn that since I Am is One,
you too will be one as We are One; Scriptures
will be fulfilled because My Sacerdotal Prayer
to the Father will be accomplished ♡ I am in
you so do not fear, This is very promising

Lord! your mission, little one, is to bring

21

My people under one Name, My Name, and break bread together ♡ there is no need to worry; do your best and I will do the rest; I need humility to accomplish My Works in you and thus bring everything on the surface; – your faithless generation, that sheds so much Blood from Me, will rebuff you, but, My Vassula, I shall hold you on your feet in spite of the impressive wounds you will receive from this evil generation; help will be given to you from above; I have preached to you and to others; do not stop there, forward the Teachings

22

I have given you both in public and in your homes ♡ I know how frail you are, but I also know what I have chosen ♡

Lord I feel content to know that we will be united, although no one yet really knows how. The problems are apparently great and the schisms greater still. As You say: "The staff of the Shepherd has been broken not only in half, but in splinters. And Your Body has been mutilated, wrenched and paralysed." You ask us all to bend. How? What is to be done? Which is the first step?
I am a greek orthodox and I am sharing with my Roman Catholic brothers everything, and I do not differentiate myself under Your Name when I am with them; nor do they treat me any differently from their own.
I also know that many of them go to the Greek or Russian Orthodox churches..

speak up, child!

23

Give me the right words Lord.

say :... and they are not allowed to share Your Body;   No. They are not allowed, although our Sacraments are the same. Yet we, orthodox are allowed to share Your Body; I was even told I was ex-communicated because I go to the R. Catholics not to say more. I am also persecuted from both sides because my confessor is a R. Catholic! And You do witness all this my Lord Jesus!

yet, the day will come when they will break bread together in one altar ♡ and no one will stop My children coming to Me ♡; no one will ask them: "are you an orthodox?*" this fortress

Apparently the greek and russian orthodox priests have the right to ask the person who wants to receive Holy Communion whether they "belong" to them. They refuse the R. Catholics from receiving Holy Communion, although the Sacraments are the same.

24

they have built to divide you is already condemned by Me; you are all brothers in Me, this is what you are to teach them to believe and persuade them to do; – as for those who remain divided in body and spirit differentiating themselves under My Holy Name I tell them as I have told the church in Sardis*: you are reputed to be alive in the eyes of the world, but not in your Maker's Eyes; revive what little you have left: it is dying fast and wherever the corpse is, there will the vultures gather;   unite! assemble! invoke My

* Ap. 3.

25

Name together! consecrate My Body and My Blood together! do not persecute the Way! humble yourselves and bend to be able to unite and glorify Me; you speak of the Spirit but do not act in the Spirit ♡ you speak of the Way but you rank first ♡ to obstruct It! — how little do you know Me .... you call out My Name, yet you murder My children between the sanctuary and the altar; I tell you solemnly, all of this will be brought to you in the Day of Judgment ♡ can you face Me and truly say: "I am

26

reconciled with My brothers;" can you truly say: "I have not differentiated myself among brothers, under Your Holy Name; I have treated them as my equal;" when you present your case before Me I shall then say to your face: "away with you, you have not treated your brothers as your equal; you have massacred daily My Body; where is your triumph? while I was building, you were tearing down, while I was reassembling you were scattering; while I was uniting you were dividing!" yet, even today, if you come to Me as

27

you are, I can heal you, I can transfigure you and you will glorify Me; "alas for those with child, or with babies at the breast, when My Day comes!" write*: alas for those I find with sin coiled in them as with child and with adepts formed by them and of their own kind ♡ but it has been said that from your own ranks there will be men coming forward with a travesty of the truth on their lips to induce the disciples to follow them (Acts 20:30) I am shouting and I

* Jesus means the explanation of this verse of Lk. 21:23

28

am trying to break through your deafness to save you, and if I reproach you it is because of the

Greatness of the Love

I have for you; but I tell you truly: I shall assemble one day all the separated parts of My Body together into One assembly; — do not weep My friend* you who love Me, endure what I endure, how- ever, console Me and have faith in Me; you will achieve great works in My Name; be

* Jesus speaks to those who truly love Him and are truly and sincerely working to unite the Churches. His friends.

29

tolerant as I am tolerant; I had been hungry,
thirsty and often starving and you came to
My help; carry on your good works and I
shall reward you; I tell you truly, you are not
alone, I am with you; be united in Me and
live in peace; you are the posterity of My Blood
and the heir of My Kingdom; tell them that
the Heart of the Lord is Love and that
the Heart of the Law is based on Love;
tell My people that I do not want administrators in My House, they will not be justified
in My Day; because it is these very ones who

30

have industrialized My House ♡ I have sent you
My Spirit to live in your hearts, this is
why the Spirit that lives in you will show
you that My Church will be rebuilt inside
your hearts and you will acknowledge each
other as your brother in your heart;

*   - will I, brother, one more season
go through the pain I have been
going through year after year?
or will you give Me rest
this time?
am I going to drink one more

31

season the Cup of your division?
or will you rest My Body
and unify, for My sake,
the Feast of Easter?
in unifying the date of Easter, you will alleviate
My pain, brother, and you will rejoice in Me
and I in you; ♡ and I will have the sight
of many restored; " my Beloved! my Creator!
He who is my husband has revealed to us things

* My Jesus, in saying all this, had taken the voice of a
victim. Weary, begging, as though He depended on us.
- Like a prisoner in a cell going to the door of his cell
and asking the guard, from the little window, how much
longer yet was his sentence, before the day of his liberation.

32

that no human hand could have performed!"
this is what you will cry out, once your sight is
restored, in My Name ♡

-    and I will come to you *
I solemnly tell you: summon, assemble all of you,
and listen this time to your Shepherd:
I will lead you in the way that
you must go;
send My Message to the ends of the earth ♡
courage, daughter, smile when I smile; I am
with you to guide your steps to heaven ΙΧΘΥΣ

* Jesus said this as a King, majestically.

33
17.10.91

Message given to the "reapers" God selected in the United States to print this book.

I give you all My Peace and bless you; I am with you to uphold your work in My Name and which I have blessed, for this is the work assigned to you all to glorify Me,

— in time of famine
I came —

to fill your mouths with My Celestial Manna so that you will not perish; I will never desert you; Love will return as Love

ΙΧΘΥΣ 🐟

34

and our Blessed Mother also gives them a message:

ecclesia will revive; glory be to God; I am the Queen of Heaven, your Mother and I bless you; pray for peace, pray for faith, love and unity; pray for the conversion of all My children; I want everybody to be saved; God's works of Light cannot be hidden forever,* this is why I have chosen you to be God's reapers ♡ I love you all with a great love and ♡ I thank you for dedicating the

* That is because of the many obstacles Satan had put to stop the Messages of the Sacred Heart from spreading.

35

Lord's Books to Me*; have faith little ones, the Lord is with you ♡ follow Him; be confident for I am with you; come;

20.10.91

Message from the Sacred Heart to Belgium. Read out in Bruxelles at St. Michael's Hall of the Jesuits' College, on the 20th.10.91.

My Lord, be with me.

feel confident because I Am is with you; My Vassula tell them this:

if many have forgotten My Sacred Heart, I have never forgotten them ♡

* The group who printed the English Books, dedicated one of them to our Blessed Mother.

36

I have called them, assembling them here today to pray together; I desire My children united; I desire My entire Church to be united; those that persist in remaining separated have already separated My Heart from theirs; realize the gravity of your division, the urgency of My Call and the importance of My request; I need your heart to unite you, and rebuild My Church united into one inside your heart; all I ask is love, to break the barriers of your division; pray, you who have offered Me your heart and

37

unite your heart with My Sacred Heart for the unity of My Churches; I, the Lord, bless each one of you leaving the Sign of My Love on your forehead; I Jesus love you

IXΘYΣ ⳨

21.10.91

Your Mercy, O Lord, has breathed in me, and inspired a living Spirit within me, in the very core of where It dwells; it was Your Word, Lord, which heals all things that healed me. And the invisible God became suddenly visible to me. And the dimness of my eyes saw a Light, a pillar of Blazing Fire, to guide my steps to Heaven. And the Darkness that imprisoned me and terrified my soul was overpowered by The Morning Star, and gave my soul Hope, Love and Peace and a great consolation, because I knew that Love and

38

Compassion Himself was my Holy Companion for the journey of my life.

My child, Love is with you and no power from beneath can or will ever separate you from Me; walk in My Light and remain united to Me ♡

22.10.91

Jesus, dress me in humility, purity and observation to Your Law, for this will please the Father.

peace be with you; for this I tell you:
be like the publican ♡
for many of you condemn your neighbour, forgetting how only yesterday, you too, were

39

locked in the same sleep; do not say:
" I have made my house tidy and ready for the Lord; He may come now to me anytime; I am ready to receive Him; I am not like my neighbour, who does not fast, does not pray, but goes on living a wicked life;" receive your sight I tell you, your lips have already condemned you; cure yourself first and do not condemn the others who do not know their left hand from their right hand; come to Me like the publican and ask Me to be merciful to you, the sinner,*

* Greek Rosary

40

for you are all subjects to sin; Temple! rise and serve Me your God, by helping the widow* you will be serving Me; go now in Peace, I am with you; ♡ Glory be to God.

24.10.91

Lord, allow me to serve You. This is my due to You now. You are known for Your Mercy and I know that if I cling to You, You will not just shake me off; I know You will rescue me.

"-I have only to open my mouth for You to fill it." Ps. 81: 11
Please feed me with Your Manna.*²

* That is, my mother. God made a point not to call her 'mother' since the only mother we have is our Blessed Mother. I'm supposed to leave and go shopping for food with her.
*2 The Holy Spirit

41

remain in My favour; I am not a God who cannot be moved ♡ My Heart is filled with Compassion and I allow Myself to be touched; come, I am your shield in these times of battle;

Lord, I am numbered among those who are violently attacked by Satan. How can Your people hear of Your marvels in the dark? The devil wants to paralyse all Your Plan! For how long yet Your Righteousness will lie in a land of oblivion? Show now, Lord of Mercy and of Justice that You are our help and consolation.

you need not fear; in the end Our Hearts will prevail ♡ I will show everyone how I can save; Scriptures have to be accomplished; you see it is written* that the beast that

* Ap. 11: 7

42

comes out of the Abyss is going to make war on the Two Lamps that stand before the Lord of the world, those Two Witnesses who represent My Body and are My Body, those that have proven they are My servants, by their great fortitude in times of suffering, trials and persecution, those who carry My Word and are My mouthpieces, and those who have been given the Truth to be as angels and an echo of the Word, since they have allowed My Spirit to be their Guide giving each one of them an Elijah ministry ♡ the appeal that they

43

make in My Name is in fact My appeal through them, they raise their voices to remind you of My Law, like Moses on the mountain at Horeb, but it is I, through them, that speak, and although for the people of the world these Two Prophets* will appear as overcome by the Enemy, I, shall breathe life into them and they will stand up; "for as the earth makes fresh things grow, as a garden makes seeds spring up, so will I, the Lord, make both integrity and praise spring up in the sight of the nations" (Is. 61: 11) I will

* Elijah and Moses: the spirit of prophecies. (The spirit of)

44

transfigure your wretched bodies into copies of My glorious Body ♡ then you will see a new heaven and a new earth sprout up; the first earth and the first heaven shall disappear, that is: the old City known by the symbolic names Sodom and Egypt, for My Word was crucified again within her,* because the people of the world did not recognize Me again, although I came to My own Domain, My own people again did not accept Me but treated My Holy Spirit as they pleased allowing the Beast to make war on those I have sent; these two cities in one, represent Sodom

Ap. 11: 8

45

and Egypt's rejection they had of My Messengers and the total deafness similar to the stubbornness of Pharaoh; these cities will be replaced by the New Jerusalem; from Sodom and Egypt you shall be called:

— New Jerusalem —

City of Integrity, City of Holiness; and when this will happen, the survivors, overcome with fear, would only praise Me*; the earth now is pregnant and in labour, My child, crying aloud in the pangs of childbirth; but the time of waiting is very soon over; I am already

* Ap. 11: 13

46

breathing on you creation reviving you one after the other, purifying you all; so if anyone has objected, he has not been objecting to you, but to Me, I who have given you My Holy Spirit of Truth, and if they recrucified anyone between the two cities by the symbolic names Sodom and Egypt, they recrucified My Word; but after three-and-a half days,* My Two Lamps will give out a brighter Light, because it will come from the brightness that surrounds the Spirit ♡ so have hope

* Ap. 11: 11 Symbolic number

47

My child; the pledge of My Spirit is for your times ♡ you are part of My Household, ecclesia shall revive ☧

24. 10. 91

Message for the Philippines :

peace be with you; tell My people to reflect upon My Law; write :

— I am reconciling the world —

tell them that it is I, Jesus; should they ask what is My Message for them, tell them:

— I am coming to reconcile you to My Sacred Heart —

48

and in reconciling you to Myself, I will ask you for the sake of My great Love to reconcile with one another; I intend to reconcile the world to My Sacred Heart and thus make a new creation out of you all*

<u>this is the pledge of My Spirit</u>

I tell you solemnly, he who sows the seeds of self-indulgence will reap a harvest of corruption and when he faces Me in the Day of Judgment I will tell him:

" go! away from Me; go to the

* Ap. 21. 1

49

Corrupt one who corrupted you ! "

<u>unless I hear a cry of repentance</u>
the smell of death that leads to death will
continue to rise all the way to heaven, I want
no more of this, what I desire from you is :

- <u>incense</u> -

I desire you to be like an incense bowl filled
with incense, on an altar, beloved children, let
your country be transformed into a huge Altar
offering Me the fragrance of incense ♡ I want
you to live holy since I am Holy ♡
each day I stretch out My Hands towards you

50

to lift you to Me; I have shown My Love for
you through ages and today, again, like a shepherd rescuing his sheep from the lion's mouth
I come to rescue you from the Viper ♡ I shall
in spite of your appalling wretchedness not overthrow you as I overthrew Sodom and Gomorrah,
I know how oppressed your needy are and how
the poor are crushed daily ; I know too how
miserable you are and oh ! I know your crimes...
and they are many, due to the violence done to
your sons the innocent blood shed in your
country is great ! your misfortunes acquired

51

from sin have challenged My Mercy and for the
sake of the greatness of My Love I call your
people today together ; summon everyone under
My Holy Name and tell them that I do not
put anyone on trial, neither do I come to me-
nace you ; tell your people that I shall outpour
My Spirit of Love upon them ; like a veil from
above I shall spread over your country and like
mist My Spirit of Love shall envelop you,
and penetrate even from the hinges of your doors
and windows ; your people will not be disappoin-
ted of My Visit ♡ I shall with My Purifying

52

Fire devour corruption and like a reaper I shall
put in My Sickle and cut this harvest of evil,
tie it together into a bundle and thrust it into
the fire to be burnt ; and in its place I shall
sow seeds from Heaven : seeds of Love ♡ this is
your Lord speaking, this is the One who loves
you more than any man can understand ;

it is I, Jesus, your Saviour,
at your doors now ; and I tell you again :
come ! come to Me, you who are oppressed, I
shall comfort you and console you, come ! come
and have all the Treasures of My Sacred Heart ;

53

the Kingdom of God* is among you, you only
have to step inside it; My House is your house;
I have opened the door to My Kingdom for everyone ♡ come, do not be tempted by violence anymore, repay evil with love —

<u>forgive!</u>

how else will the Father forgive <u>you</u> if you are
not willing to forgive? eat from My fruit and not
from the fruit of My enemy, for the children of
darkness are wicked in dealing even with their own
kind because Evil is their master who teaches
them to be like him and the man who is

* That is the Church.

54

dishonest in little things will be dishonest in
greater things too ♡ call together your friends
and pray; I shall hear your prayer:

— <u>every repentant sinner will be heard</u> —

— <u>in Heaven</u> —

I Jesus bless you all leaving the Sigh of My Love
on your forehead ♡ ΙΧΘΥΣ ⤳ ◯

25.10.91

Lord?

I Am ♡

Lord, bind me to You even more now and keep me
away from insults of men because I live ecu-
menically. Bind me to Your Heart and when I
walk let Your Light be my Guide. When I

55

lie down let Your Spirit watch over me and when
I wake up make my spirit talk to Your Spirit.
Let me act like You and court You. Make
my heart eager to seek You so that I pay
everything I vowed to You.
Remind us all, Lord, what You had given
us. You had given us One sturdy Holy Church
filled with Your Holy Spirit not an empty rubble,
You had given us One solid Staff, not two or
three or a heap of splinters, where has all
this gone?

Vassula, let Me tell you first: the insults of
those who insult you fall on Me — so do not
give up, carry My Cross of Unity from nation
to nation and be My Echo ♡ to refresh the
memories of My people I am sending My Holy
Spirit to remind them to adopt a mutual love

56

that leads to peace and a mutual understanding; —
in My preliminary Messages about Unity I had
asked you all to bend, but have I today
anyone who is ready to listen to what My
Spirit says?

— is there among you any good man left?

— is there anyone who really looks for Me?

— has anyone yet lowered his voice to hear
Mine?

— who is the first righteous man among you
who will decline and fade away so that
My Presence be seen?

57

- who among you is ready to lower his head
and allow My Head to be revealed?

- is there any generous man among you who will
lower his voice and hear My supplicating
prayer to the Father:

" Am I, Father

to drink one more season of
the Cup of their division?
or will they at least unify the Feast
of Easter
alleviating part of My
pain and sorrow?

58

will this reign of
Darkness
last much longer?
they have severed My Body
and have forgotten that it is
My Head
which strengthens and holds the
whole Body
together;
O Father!
reconcile them,
and remind them

59

that by My death on
the Cross
I have given them My Peace;
give them the Spirit of Truth
in its fulness
into their hearts,
and when they see their nakedness
they will understand;
forgive them Father
for they know not what they
are doing; "

60

The Citadel
of the proud shall
fall into a heap of dust
My Child *
their pride and glory will fall when My Spirit
besieges them; - just wait and you shall see ♡
write: are you really listening? are you
really listening to what I am saying? what
I am saying to you, means Peace, for My
own and for My friends, they would

* Here I had the impression the Father was answering.

61

understand if they, from today, renounce their folly; for those who love Me without reserve, and who fear Me, My saving help is at hand's reach, and the glory will then live in each one of you; Love and Loyalty can meet, Right- eousness and Peace can embrace; Loyalty can reach up from earth for Righteousness always leaned from heaven; I have been bestowing you happiness, what has your soil given as harvest? Righteousness always preceded Me and Peace followed My Footsteps; am I to say the same for you? who will make up for the years of your

62

division? solemnities and discourses do not interest Me; pretence and lip-service do not deceive Me either; oh daughter, what I wish them to understand, especially those who live in My Wounds is that My sorrow is great, and the reason why I have put some things rather strongly, is to enable them to preach some- thing of the Spirit and not of the letter; I want to fill their spirit with My Tran- scendent Light so that they see things with My Eyes and not with theirs; to see things with My Divine Light and not

63

theirs; I am known to be Faithful and Righteous and it does not mean because they lack fidelity and righteousness, I too will show them less Fidelity, Righteousness and Peace, and not come to rescue them; - even if all of them turn away from Me and from My Ways, I will remain Faithful and True *; My Spirit will be at work restoring Peace among brothers and through My Cross and My Wounds I will unite you all in one single Body and have you glorify Me around

* Ap. 19:11

64

One Single Tabernacle

and the barrier which keeps you apart will be broken; the ban will be lifted * and My Sacrificial Throne will be in its place ♡ come to Me as little children that I may open the eyes of your soul that you may see what Hope My Call holds for

you ♡

bless Me daughter, ♡ come ΙΧΘΥΣ ⊂⊃

I bless You Lord. 'Bring forward the people that is blind, yet has eyes, that is deaf and yet has ears. Let all the nations muster and assemble with every race. Let men hear You so that they may say: 'It is true'.' (Is. 43:8-9)

* Ap. 22.3

29. 10. 91

My God !

I Am ; alone you are not ; I am present and
with you ; Nassula, allow Me to speak to you,
have faith in Me, I am near you, come,
concentrate and meditate on Me, work for My
Glory ♡ daughter, tell them* in this way :
"blessed are the poor in spirit for
theirs is the kingdom of heaven ; you are
all very precious to Me ; pray more than
ever before and I will supply the wretched,
I will heal the blind and teach each one of
you My Law from the stranger to your own ;

* The people I would be meeting
in England.

Love loves you ΙΧΘΥΣ 〜

(This is a preliminary message, as an introduction
for my whole trip in England.)

Later on :

Nassula, be constant in your prayers, I love you
My child and oh ! do I know your weaknesses
daughter, bring My children to the real faith
bring everyone to Me, this is part of your
mission too ♡ ah My child, be fervent for Me
your Lord ;

My Lord, not everyone listens to these messages
when I proclaim them. Is it possible that
they have not understood ? I am not only
talking for myself I am also talking about
the present apparitions and about others

You've used as Your instruments in a supernatural
way. I will put it to You directly : how
many in the high hierarchy today lend an ear
and are positive ? How many ?
and how many of the high priests and scribes
lent an ear to Me and were positive, only yesterday ? — Nassula, there is a remnant chosen
by grace to believe ♡ Scriptures say : I revealed
Myself to those who did not consult Me (Rm 10:20)
yet from the very beginning I have invited
everyone to My School ;

My Holy Spirit is your Guide,

your Husband* and your

* Allusion to Is. 54:5

- Master -

I tell you truly that soon I will gather all
nations in a circle of Love and My Spirit
will dwell in you giving sight to the blind,
since the Light that will be given you is : My
Transcendent Light ; but how hard it is for
those who have accumulated riches in their
spirit to penetrate into My Light ! how hard
it is for the wise to penetrate into the Spirit
and perceive Its depths ! how hard it is for
them to enter into My Kingdom ! I tell you
solemnly, the rejects of your society and those

5

you call unworthy are making it before them;
yes! those who could not tell good from evil,
those who could not tell their left hand from
their right! I have been and am still inviting
everyone to sit at table with Me, but many
have not responded to My invitation, they
laughed and scorned at My Gracious Call
and caused others who wanted to come, stumble
by their teaching ♡ compare all this with My
parable of the wedding feast (Mt. 22:1-14)
I will come back*
and they will tremble; they will tremble when

* Second Pentecost: The outpour of the Spirit: Joël 3

6

they will realize whom they were rejecting all this
time; they renounced My Spirit and allowed
themselves to be guided by their own spirit,
they renounced My Light for their own, they
renounced My Heavenly Knowledge given by
Wisdom for a second-rate philosophy and
their own rational knowledge;
- they have apostatised -
since they have rejected My Spirit, My
Light and My Knowledge; I shall take
away My Kingdom from them and give it
to a people who can produce its fruit; I

7

shall then welcome these people as My own
and ask them to come with Me and keep
house with Me; in fact this hour is here
already; I have decided to draw near Me the
disreputable, those that hang around on every
street corner, the unworthy, the nothing of
the nothings, the wretched and those who
never knew My Name; I will turn to a wretched
lot who never loved Me and make a nation
of Love out of them, a holy nation, and they
will glorify Me ♡ they will be called priests
of the Living God, priests of the Amen, and

8

in this priesthood I shall rebuild My Church,
in these hearts I shall unite you all, and
My Body will rest ♡ the hour is here, and
no one can stop this hour of My Holy Spirit;
when you will see the world disintegrating under
your feet, when you will look to your left
and see tottering kingdoms and cities reduced
into a heap of dust, and to your right
mountains tumbling, know that these signs
are the beginning of the outpouring of My Holy
Spirit; when you see My pupils whom I
Myself have formed, preach fearlessly in My

9

Name, do not disrupt them, resist your temp-
tation and discern the sound of their footsteps,
I will keep sending you these saints to gather
on their way all the severed members of My
Body, and no one, not even the unclean
spirits would be able to stop them, these will
instead fall down before them because they will
know that the Amen is their Master ♡

the Amen is soon

with you My child

He who is your Consoler

and whose Home is in inaccessible light

10

will eventually plunge you into His

light and absorb you;

– I am Love ♡ –

Blessed be Your glorious and Holy Name, praised
and extolled for ever.

5. 11. 91

England- Manchester - (Just before going to
the meeting in St. Augustine's Church the devil
attacked me with the aim to spoil the meeting.
I prayed to St. Michael twice and I prayed two
decades of the Rosary, to Rosa Mystica.) (The
devil's grip released.) – Our blessed Mother
then gives me this message.)

I am with you My child; do not fear,
I will not leave you an inch from My
sight; work in peace, Vassula; I love you,

11

pray now and go in peace and remember I
am with you ♡

6. 11. 91

England- Before going to Strangeways Prison to read
to them their message.

My child all the strength you will receive
will come from Me; show, My child, what
the Lord says to the world; show them
how My Eyelids run with weeping; let
My people pray for those who do not invoke
My Name and I shall cure them; the
impossible will become possible; the desert
will turn into a garden and the rubble into

12

an altar for Me your God; tell My children
to pray; pray with their heart and I shall
listen ♡ I call all those who are crushed
with pain to offer Me their pain and rest in
My Heart; I shall help them carry their
cross; so My Vassula feel My Presence; see Me
with the eyes of your soul; speak to Me
and allow Me to use you to glorify Me ♡

England- Manchester　　　　　　　　　　8. 11. 91

peace be with you; My purpose for descending
in this way is for your salvation; what I
have commenced and blessed I shall finish;

13

tell My children that when I speak to them, using you as a means, I mean Salvation, I mean Peace, I do not mean destruction; but the devil <u>means</u> destruction, for what he means kills; Faithful Love leans all the way down from heaven to reach you and offer you His Heart ♡ you are all so very precious to Me; the Holy One is revealing His Face: I call each one of you without any distinctions; you are all Mine and you all belong to Me and your life is in My Hands perpetually; do not be like those who seem to talk about Unity

14

but yet draw a sword for the ones who prac- tise it; come to Me as one family and we shall all sup together, I and you, you and I; I am allowing everyone to hear My Voice; I bless you all; adorn Me with prayers from your heart ΙΧΘΥΣ 〜〜

9.11.91

(Manchester -) Lord?

I Am; little one be blessed, there still are a few more things I wish to write through you; so allow Me to use you ♡ think, daughter, what you have earned as Knowledge from Me; I will reinforce My temple* so that its

* Jesus means, me.

15

structure becomes solidly strong and will re- main unscathed from any blow that may come upon it; I shall increase in you and not decrease; let My Spirit rest in you; the Holy One gives you His Peace ♡

13.11.91

Yahweh I love You. I adore You. Yahweh, my celestial Love I know you are with me. Yahweh my Father and Abba, tell Your so- Beloved Son that my heart lives for Him only. Tell Him that He is the Air I breathe, My Life. Tell Him that my voice for His Sake will be carried as far as I can, to proclaim His Desires and His Fervent Love for us. <u>Tell</u> Him Father that no one and nothing will <u>ever</u> come between this love I have for Him. Tell Him that He is my Smile, my Joy and my Hope. Tell my Re- deemer how I long for Him and how I pine

16

away with love for Him day and night. daughter, beloved of My Soul, did you not know? did you not know how My Spirit reposes on Nothingness? have you not heard how I delight revealing My entire Face to children? have you not read: "I have been found by those who did not seek Me and have revealed Myself to those who did not consult Me"; (Rom. 10:20) - your Joy is your Maker, - your Love is your Anointed One, - your Torch is My Holy Spirit; benefit, My child, from all the gifts I

17

have given you and restore My House; I happened
to be taking a walk nearby a river when I
saw a driftwood*, drifting away with the
worldly current; I leaned over and picked it
out of the stream, I brought it Home with
Me and planted it in My Garden of Delights;
from a dry piece of wood I made out of
you a Tree; I said : " grow ! grow and take
root in My Garden, in My own Property;
and from your blossoms exhale a perfume to
appease My Justice;" I said : " crops of fruit
shall sprout each month and your leaves

* God means me.

18

will be the cure to many;" now and then I
amuse Myself in pruning you; My delight is
to see flowers in blossom and a constant growth
in your fruit ♡ alone, the Water*¹ from My
Sanctuary*² can give you growth and Life ;
I, Yahweh, will see to it that you
prosper; I take pleasure in picking now and
then on My way pieces of driftwood;*³ I can
give life to anything I pick on My way;

☧

*¹ That is the Holy Spirit.
*² That is the Heart of the Lord.
*³ God was hinting to me of another privileged soul He
allowed me to meet.

19

13. 11. 91

Vassula, peace be with you; — if the
earth will shake and wither under their
very eyes it will be because they have trans-
gressed My Law which is based on Love;
they have violated all My Commandments;
in spite of the multiple intercessions of your
Holy Mother and in spite of My Warnings,
from the time in Fatima to this epoch, none
of My Warnings have been respected; the hours
are fleeing and a mighty host such as the
world has never seen, nor will ever see again
is at hand ! few men will be left; how

20

I shout to break through your deafness !
a nation roaring like the roar of many
waters will flood the world again, with
fire and brimstone; I am rich in forgiving,
but I hardly hear any cry of repentance;
oh men of little faith ! men of arguments
only ! write: all I hear except from only
a remnant is : " why should we have to
believe in messages ? why should we fast since
these are not from Him ? why do penance since
we are righteous ? why should we believe this
frenzied lot ? do not listen for they

21

retail visions and prophecies of their own";
I tell you truly, when that Day comes it
would have been preferable you were never born!
it takes only one man to blow a fire to
produce any heat; today again a man is
among you living under the same skies who
is ready to blow a Fire that can burn and
melt all elements within a matter of seconds!
the earth, like a garment will wear out;
I had warned you, but you paid no heed;
My suffering is great but how else am I to
expel the merchants from within My Church?

22

how am I to throw out the vipers from their
nests inside My Sanctuary if I am not to come
with Flame and a Blazing Fire? traders,
merchants, the lot will be extirpated and this
could be done only by Fire! the sages will
boast no more of their wisdom nor of their
authority; the rich in spirit will be laid
barren and naked and they will mourn;
they will look for Me but where they look
they will not find Me; they will invoke My
Name again and again but I shall not hear
them; I shall overthrow the lot ♡

23

be one with Me My child, have My Peace, I
love you very much; justice is at hand ✶

Later on:

lean on Me; I am with you My child; ah
My little child, carry for My sake your bur-
den upon your shoulders; love Me My child
and you shall live; evangelize with love for
love; accept all that comes from Me; come, I
and you, you and I united in love; I love you
so much, My Vassula, so much little one ...

ecclesia will revive ΙΧΘΥΣ ⊰⊱⊝

24

14.11.91

Message for Ireland.
listen, Ireland, disperse no more, assemble,
assemble all in one; come to Me in peace, and
pray together for peace; empty your hearts of
all your evil inclinations and learn where
peace is, where love is, where sanctity is ♡
pray for those whose hands are dripping
with blood, they know not what they are
doing; I have come to take aside the best of
the flock to ask them if they are willing to
make a general renunciation of nine days;
the demons in this country will be panic-

25

stricken; I know that your crimes are many and that only a remnant have My Seal on their forehead; I have passed through you, Ireland, and I have staggered in your lawlessness,

but look! the Hour is at Hand; your land is parcelled by a measuring line but so is your heart Ireland My daughter, right down to your entrails;* re-erect My tottering House by assembling in peace and without differentiating yourselves under My Name; even though you are a remnant faithful to Me,

* God is talking of the different denominations of His Church.

26

be not discouraged, I shall bring you new wine with a blessing to moisten your lips; be not discouraged; your Saviour is on His way of Return; you are the bricks of My Sanctuary and at the same time the builders of My House; by uniting and reassembling, there will be a structure, but if you remain divided and scattered how am I to reconstruct what is in ruin now? I need you all together to make one unity and reconstruct My House ♡ I need all the bricks; My Kingdom on earth is My Church and the Eucharist

27

is the Life of My Church, this Church I Myself have given you; - I had left you with one Church, but hardly had I left, just barely had I turned My back to go to the Father, than you reduced My House to a desolation! you levelled it to the ground! and My flock is straying left and right ... for how long am I to drink of the Cup of your division? cup of affliction and devastation; you have offered the Holy One, the One you say you love a cup that is so wide and so deep, filled with bitterness and

28

sorrow that My palate is drier than parchment, My lips covered with blisters; the flavour of this cup this generation is offering Me is as bitter as venom; I am not alone to swallow My Tears, your Holy Mother is sharing My grief, since Her Immaculate Heart is united in love to My Sacred Heart ♡ but soon I shall renew you all with My Fire; pray without ceasing, for the Hour is at hand; I bless you all sealing your foreheads with the Sign of My Love ΙΧΘΥΣ

29

My Lord?

I Am, come to Me at all times; pray with Me, say:

You are my only God,
my only Hope,
my only Love,
You are my God unrivalled
ever so Tender and Delicate
with the weak and the wretched,
let not the Chalice of Your Justice
brim over us;
allow the captives to be set free

30

before Your Day my Lord,
our faults in Your Eyes have been many
and our rebellion and apathy even greater
in number,
but Your Heart is throbbing
with Love and Compassion,
give us O Father, most Gracious,
a powerful Breath of Your Spirit
to revive us all
for Your Glory ♡ amen
I bless you, My child ♡ ♡

31

Jesus? Holy One?

I Am; little one, daughter of Mine peace be with you, I, the Lord, bless you and bless you; evangelize with love for Love; tell them that I love each one of them in a special way; tell them also that I am not a complicated God; I am not far; I am present at this very moment; tell them how I long for their love; show them what the Lord's Heart is; tell them that the Lord's Heart is nothing else but Love and Mercy and if Justice is brought down upon you it is because of the

32

graveness of your sins and crimes; how many times I overlook all that you do not do in My favour and how many times I kept away the Father's Hand from falling upon you! Jesus is My Name and Jesus means Saviour; I am the Saviour of all mankind ♡

ΙΧΘΥΣ ><>

Ireland - Cork - 22.11.91

beloved children, I give you My Peace, the world is falling into decay, but I have not forgotten you; I am visiting you in your distress to help each one of you reach your Room

33

in Heaven ; you are Mine and you are all very precious to Me ;

I am the Light of the world, so do not fear, I ask you to pray for those who have hardened their heart and do not believe in the Truth ; never cease your prayers ; I, the Lord, have passed through your cities, Ireland, and although at the moment you do not know the Plans I have designed for you ; - remain in My Divine Love and you shall feel strong,

remain in My Sacred Heart and you shall prosper,

remain in My favour by your constancy and faith,

34

- remain in Me, and you shall live ; I, the Lord, bless each one of you leaving the Sign of My Love on your forehead ; remember : Love loves you ;

ΙΧΘΥΣ ⊃⊂=Ð

24. 11. 91

My child, I am the only Mother of all mankind ; every single one of you is My child ;

Holy Mother will every one, one day accept this Truth ?

in the end every soul will accept this truth ; those who sincerely love God now, will accept it ; never cease praying My child for the conversion of the world ; understand that

35

the more prayers I obtain the less evil will be promulgated ; prayers are never wasted ; I offer them to the Father whose Justice is at hand ; pray to obtain God's Mercy ; you do not know what God has reserved for this evil generation, but have in mind how in rebellious times His Hand fell on sinful men, and that was then, a fraction of what He has now in store for you ; His Justice will respond from His Holy Abode in accordance to the sins of this generation, He will come with Fire, thunder, hurricane and flame of devouring Fire to burn up the crimes

36

of the world ; no, you do not know what the Almighty has reserved for you to purge mankind ; the signs are there all around you, but few see or notice them ; innocent blood is shed of My sons' and daughters' for Satan ; this innocent blood is offered like a holocaust to the Evil one, Satan's plan is to strip this world from its creation, annihilate you all and engulf you all in flames ; he wants one big holocaust out of all of you ; I shout, I cry out, I shed Tears of Blood, but few pay attention ; God will be coming to you

37

but you do not know in which way;
Holy Mother, we are praying but as You say, we are very few; what to do?!

Your prayers can change the world; your prayers can obtain God's Graces for the conversion of sinners and the more conversion the more prayers will be made and heard for other conversions; do you understand? prayers are powerful; this is why I insist of you not to abandon your prayers and your sacrifices, the faithful are needed now more than ever; God will remember all your sacrifices My dearest

38

children, love Him and glorify Him ♡
ecclesia shall revive in "all Her" glory ♡

(Later on)

Lord?

I Am; delight Me and do not keep silent in proclaiming the Truth; I have blessed your mission; I am your Rock and Shelter; if you lie low My Presence shall be seen in all its splendour; you will pray, I am listening;

Lord, forgive us our guilt,

our wickedness, our failures, our intolerance,

39

our Lack of love,

forgive us the Lack of our love

and sensitivity.

Convert

the wicked, the impenetrable, the lethargic,

the atheists,

and transfigure them into vessels of light

to glorify You.

Humble the proud, lower the high,

bend the rigid;

Transfigure us all as in Your Transfiguration.

Amen.

40

once My Holy Spirit besieges you, you will all be transfigured; I am always ready to forgive you; I love you little one; we, us? yes Lord.

25.11.91

Lord, have I failed You in any way? You have called me but have I really responded You? Have I really listened to Your Voice, or have I been ignoring It? Have I maybe been insensitive to the appeals of Your Sacred Heart? Have You taken Your Loving Eyes off me O Holy of Holies?
In the anguish of my spirit, I pray and ask You:

Where are those Eyes so
Loving upon me?

Where is my Abode,
Your Sacred Heart?

41

How is it I cannot hear
Your Voice,
or feel Your Presence?

Have I lost Your Friendship
because of my insensitivity?

Have I lost Your Companionship
O Holy of Holies?

My priest! the corpse will be tossed inside a hole, buried and forgotten, daughter from Egypt, have My Peace; I have placed you in the land of the living; look at Me and be confident of My Love and Friendship I have for you; do not make Me weep out of pain, how would I desert you? but the evil one

42

is desperately trying to loot all the riches I Myself have offered you; out of the pit I have taken you and back in the pit he wants you buried; daughter, trust Me, orphaned I shall not leave you; take My guarantee, daughter; I shall never abandon you! hear Me: be reassured, you have not wasted your breath; * you are so, so weak and

* The Tempter came to me saying that I was not doing enough for the Lord and that all my meetings in England and Ireland were a total 'fiasco', and that all my words said to them were wasted. I panicked and thought the Lord had turned His back to me.

43

powerless and ah! how My Spirit can breathe freely in you! whispering in echoes I flutter at your ear My Words that are to be uttered in My Assemblies; why, soul, you are un-learned and utterly powerless for all that are Knowledge and Wisdom; so how could your spirit comprehend all of this unless the Spirit who speaks through you is My Own? Vassula* .... you are so very precious to Me .... listen My child, there is an Angel by your side to take pity on you, console you and pray for you; wait, I have more to say;

* Jesus uttered my name almost in a whisper.

44

recognize your stupendous weakness, this is why I shall use this weakness to draw My people to Unity and show them how I, the Lord, feel in their negligence; I will show them what is most desired by Me; I shall, in your weakness, show them how I feel about those distinctions they have created among them; — tell Me, are you not all alike, made by My Own Hands?   Yes Lord. who has not been made according to the likeness of My Image?   No one Lord! How does their way of thinking affect You my Lord?

45

because of man's base pride, My Father's Cup is filled with His justice, because of their rigidity they are left uninhabited! many of them talk of unity and brotherhood, but their words are fallacious, void; — prove yourselves in your Maker's Eyes by bending; prove yourselves in your Maker's Eyes by unifying the date of Easter; prove yourselves to Me by breaking bread together; robe yourselves in majesty and splendour with humility and not with an outward appearance of religion and piety; repent! — once you lived in humility

46

simplicity and unbounded love with rich food covering your table; yes, the greatness of My Church exceeded everything and every living creature, because the Eucharist made the life of My Church; — if My Church today lacks brightness it is because many of My churches have abolished My Perpetual Sacrifice*; — can one peer through this shadowed darkness and still claim they can see? can one boast of having escaped ambushes in this darkness? but "so long as you say: "we see"; your guilt remains! I have said that there are other

* Predicted by the prophet Daniel 11:31

47

sheep I have that are not of the one fold and that I have to lead as well; but no sooner do I bring a wandering lamb back to the fold to lead a True Life in Me, no sooner do I restore back his sight than you charge on him to take away the Kingdom of Heaven from him; — could a devil open the eyes of the blind? could he make him cry out 'Abba!' so, unless you repent, My Father's Hand will fall upon you; I can no longer sustain His Hand from falling; unless you forgive, each one of you, your brother <u>from your heart</u>,

48

My Father's Hand will fall more rapidly than you think; ΙΧΘΥΣ ⊂●>

(Another message for the Philippines.)   3.12.91
tell My people that they are like bricks, and I can use them for the restoration of My House; I can, if they allow Me, use each one of them; — allow Me to guide you all; abandon yourselves to Me without inquiring, why; just trust Me your Lord; offer Me your will but do not object at Me when I use it; pray with your heart, and confess your sins ♡ reflect on My Passion and all I have offered you ♡

49

4.12.91

(Before one of the meetings in the Philippines.)

Lord? I Am; fear not, I have not abandoned you; I love you; beloved daughter, your apostolate is to spread My Glorious Light in every nation; spread all that you received from Me; this, My child, is what you will have to do; the rest, I will do ♡ by doing the work I have given you I shall protect you; you have nothing to fear. I, Jesus, so much love you; - now, do not try to understand but by testing you I make your spirit grow in holiness; be at My service, child, by doing the work I have

50

given you; I shall always encourage you to witness with zeal for Me and My House, and I will always discourage you from looking to your left and to your right; I shall not be harsh with you because of your appalling misery; - since you will be serving Righteousness Himself, I will have you fastened to Me to stand firm by My Side, otherwise, alone, you will waver; - now, My Spirit, your Holy Companion will lead you with enthusiasm to My children; by grace you will speak for Me; I am with you and I shall never fail

51

you; come ♡ ΙΧΘΥΣ ><>

5.12.91

For the Philippine prayer group.

I bless all of them; tell My children that My Heart is ablaze and on fire ready to consume them; they have only to step inside My Sacred Heart and I will leave them ravished for Me their God; (then to a particular one.)

- I am today offering you My Heart; take It; Jesus is My Name and Jesus means

- Saviour -

Love loves you: and you*, My offspring,

* Jesus then turned to me.

52

continue to weave all that I have given you; empty you shall not be; look, your table is full and without Me your table will be empty: it is I who provide your soul. so cling to Me and you shall live; My Holy Kiss is on your forehead, I love you, love Me ΙΧΘΥΣ ><>

5.12.91

/For the prisoners of Muntin Lupa - in Manila, Philippines

Vassula, peace My child; say to the prisoners:
- did you not know? have you not heard how Mercy leans all the way to all mankind? Here is your God leaning all the way

53

from His Throne to reach you;

— I have come to you —

to tell you of the Great Love I have for each one of you; I am your God speaking through My instrument to give you My Message; I have come to speak to you in your heart and console you, My friends; I tell you, the world is nothing before Me, so do not fear the world, come to Me and lean on Me and I shall shepherd you to My everlasting Waters; I shall heal your wounds and dress them; My Eyes never leave you and I tell you, with Me,

54

your table shall always be full; with Me, you will sup, My friends; and when the heavy scourge comes upon you, do not let this confuse you, beloved ones; every time it comes upon you, look at My Wounds that healed you and saved you from Death; look at Me, your Saviour; do not look to your left nor to your right; follow My Footprints; you will recognize them by the trace of Blood in them; follow them, beloved ones, and they will lead you where I Am ♡ I bless each one of you leaving the Sign of My Love

55

on your foreheads; Love loves you ΙΧΘΥΣ ⊃─○

(for sister Theresa who takes care of the prisoners, and who transformed the prisoners into devout beings to God.)

I have given them a Rock and, ah!.... how I love this Rock. I the Lord bless her and bless her for she has made out of a desert where the vipers nestle,

a productive ground,

a garden, where I the Lord

can have My rest ♡

8.12.91

Lord? I Am; pray before you rest in

56

Me, say with Me:

Jesus rest in me

and I in You,

united, linked together; amen

(I repeated it) be firm about the Two Hearts, united in love; I have spoken in many hearts already about this truth, a truth that many will reject but in the end, Our Two Hearts will prevail; such is the world; today they reject, but tomorrow they will honour this truth; I Jesus love you all; have no other but Me in your heart; have Me as first;

57

have My Peace ΙΧΘΥΣ 🐟

Philippines 12.12.91
(My thoughts went to Switzerland.)
Lord, how is the church in Switzerland?

.... it is a rubble ...

Xmas Eve 24.12.91
My Lord? I Am; lean on Me, child; (I saw

with the eyes of my soul Jesus' holy Face. He
looked like a child with big innocent eyes.
tremendous reparations have to be done to
cicatrize the wounds of this earth; wounds
and cuts made by wickedness and sin; —
delight the Eyes of your Saviour and expand.
<u>let it be</u>

58

that My Message becomes so ample, so vast,
testifying itself, that Wickedness, Apathy and
Atheism will be seized and will repent ♡
child! cling to the hem of My clothes ♡
and stretch* even more now, from one corner
of the earth to the other ♡ enter into
My Sanctuaries if they welcome you into
My Sanctuaries; if men forbid you, do
not let this afflict you nor bring you
sorrow, do not despair; your oppressors will
look back in those scenes in the day of the

* Jesus means to widen the scope., in spreading this urgent message.

59

Purification and will weep ♡ remembering their
rejection; they will realize how they were
rejecting Our Divine Hearts, not you; Our
Two Hearts that prophesied; daughter, follow
My blood-stained Footprints and pronounce
My Holy Name in any gathering; <u>the time</u>
<u>has come that you should not hesitate</u>
<u>anymore</u>; plant Vineyards everywhere and
anywhere you can, make gardens out of
deserts; I have blessed My Messages to
prosper and take root, so, courage, daughter,
(Suddenly I felt a 'sword of fire' pierce me,

60

and I cried out: Lord! I miss You!)
you miss Me because you saw My Glory ....
write: — citadel after citadel is being
besieged by the Rebel; I come today and
offer all mankind My Peace but very few
listen; today I come with peace-terms and
a Message of Love, but the peace I am
offering is blasphemed by the earth and the
Love I am giving them is mocked and jeered
in this Eve of My Birth; mankind are
celebrating these days without My Holy Name;
My Holy Name has been abolished and they

61

take the day of My Birth as a great holiday of leisure, worshipping idols; Satan has entered into the hearts of My children, finding them weak and asleep; I have warned the world; Fatima's Message speaks:

that in My Day I shall make the sun go down at noon and darken the earth in broad daylight; I will allow the Dragon to bite this sinful generation and hurl a Fire the world has never seen before or will ever come to see again, to burn her innumerable crimes; you will ask: "will

62

all the inhabitants perish, the good with the bad?" I tell you: the living will envy the dead; out of two men one will be taken; some will ask: "where are Elijah and Moses who are to come?" I tell you, you evil generation: We* have not been speaking in parables all these years; Elijah and Moses have come already and you have not recognized them but treated them as you pleased; you have not listened to Our Two Hearts, the Immaculate Heart of My

* Christ means the Two Hearts who are the two witnesses in Ap. 11. 1-13 and in Zc 4: 1-14

63

Mother and My Sacred Heart, you faithless generation ... Our Two Hearts have not been speaking to you in parables nor in riddles; all Our Words were Light and Our Hearts like Two Lamps are shining near each other so bright, that everyone may see ♡♡ but, you have not understood; Our Hearts, like Two Olive Trees*¹ one to the right and one to the left were for so many years trying to revive you; like Two Olive Branches pouring oil*² to heal your sick generation

*¹ Ap. 11: 4 + Zc. 4: 3   *² Zc. 4: 12

64

and cicatrize your wounds, but your generation treated Our Two Hearts as they pleased; Our Two Hearts are anointed*¹ and are living, They are like a sharp sword, double-edged,*² prophesying, but the rebellious spirit in this generation is recrucifying My Word*³ the double-edged sword, and are rejecting Our Two Hearts who speak to you today; just like Sodom's and Egypt's rejection of My messengers; this era's stubbornness has surpassed Pharaoh's, because their claims

*¹ Zc 4: 14   *² Ap. 1: 16   *³ Allusion to Ap. 11: 8-10

to their knowledge have become a battle-
field to My Knowledge*¹, indeed Our Two
Hearts have become a plague to the people
of the world*², but soon, very soon now,
My Voice shall be heard again, I shall
visit you by thunder and fire; Justice is
at hand; and Our Two Hearts you have
combated shall prevail in the end*³; and
the kingdom of the world will become My
Kingdom*⁴; this is all very close now;

* ¹ Allusion to Ap. 11:7   * ² Ap. 11:10
* ³ Allusion to Ap. 11:11 * ⁴ Ap. 11:15

open your eyes and look around you; I
am giving you all the signs of the Times;
and you, you who are labouring to bring
to the surface the devotion of the Alliance
of the Two Hearts, do not lose courage;
the Book of Apocalypse speaks as well
as the Book of Zechariah of this Truth;
do not fear, spread this devotion with
trust and with courage;

$$\alpha \, ✗ \, \Omega$$

16.1.92

O Lord, I cannot find words to praise You,
yet I want to talk to You ...

I shall help you, write:

Yahweh visited me,

like a gust of wind

His Spirit lifted me

and showed me

His Countenance,

He revealed to me:

Tenderness, Love and

Infinite Goodness,

He then showered me with Blessings

and offered me Manna in abundance

to share it with my brothers;

He walked with me in the land of oblivion,

from down among the dead

He took me,

among those who have forgotten Him

He raised me

restoring the memory of my soul;

O Lord, Yahweh, how grateful I am!

may Your Sweetness O Lord

be on us all,

Blessed be Yahweh

5

for ever and ever; Amen
and now, daughter, the terrors of the night
are behind you and before you, I Am ♡
I shall bring you safely Home, back
where you belong; α/ω

17.1.92
Lord of Mercy, your people need to be consoled,
Your 'Body', 'divided', is sinking and there
are very few who can comfort You, Your
people are in despair, listen, therefore, Lord
of Mercy and see our sorrow. Amen.

soaked in My Blood I am from all that
My Eyes are witnessing and from what My
Ears are hearing; daughter, I mean to

6

make you the sword of My Word, through
you I shall pierce hearts of men to allow My
Word to penetrate profoundly in them;
My Voice shall echo in them and though
their heart has not a breath of life inside
it, My Word, the giver of Life, will
revive it and from it will issue a fragrance,
appeasing My Wounds; daughter of Mine,
courage; many will continue to live an
unholy life and many will continue sinning
and offending My Holiness, heedless of My
warnings, heedless of the signs I am

7

giving the world today and wickedness will
go on increasing My Cup of Justice ♡
wickedness and atheism, thirst of power and
rationalism are worn like a signet ring on
these men; ah, My Vassula, ... there will be
a loss such as never seen! the sinner lurks
for his chance and like a prowler, he shall
come by night! multiple will be the wails,
from rulers, magistrates and influential men,
all will wail! My daughter, hear My
sighs, listen to My Heart; O beloved of
My Soul, come and console My Heart;

8

hunger for Me, I am the Resurrection, love
Me; let your prayers be an advocate to defend your generation from My Father's wrath,
let your cries and your prayers be like a
plea to the Father; I, the Lord, bless
you, child, come .... A/Ω

18.1.92
(First day of the week of Unity.)

Give us Lord Your discerning
Spirit,
To gain Knowledge and Wisdom,
Give us Yahweh the ear
of the humble and the lowly
to search for Your Knowledge
and Wisdom.

Give Your Church her triumph

9

by uniting us all in
one Body. Amen

evangelize with love for Love; live for Me,
breathe for Me; all that I have said to you
shall soon take place; you shall see more
wonders through Me; the panoply is not
yet worn by My Church ♡ the crown of
triumph soon will be worn, adorning
Her victory; — I love you for giving Me
your time, and offering it so generously to
Me; We love you*; it makes Me happy

* The Holy Trinity spoke.

10

to know that you want to share My Work
with Me; have My Peace ΙΧΘΥΣ 🐟

20.1.92

(For the Swiss group.)

this prolonged silence from My part* would
not have lasted had I been approached
with love; how can they claim they love Me
when they have no peace nor any love among
them? like a wasting sickness sin devours
them; My Magnificence has not penetrated
them nor has My Splendour; I came to

* Jesus had eclipsed Himself for some time in
Switzerland.

11

water their aridity with My Tears; I came
to console them, yet have I received any
in return? their cities* are empty with empti-
ness and a rubble today; like drought in
a dry land they became; My Word has
come to their ear, yet they did not hear
it; My Throne of Grace approached them
and offered them My Peace and sound
Teaching from Wisdom Herself to set them
free and yet, they did not share it with
faith nor love; anyone who claims to be
in the light but hates his brother,

* souls

12

hates Me ♡ the original request which was
given to them in My Message was

love, peace, unity
and reconciliation among brothers;
now all I have to say is:

examine yourselves before Judgement comes,
you have very little time left now; pray
and avoid all evil; never condemn or
judge one another; set your hearts for Me;
set your minds on Me; stay awake for
the cleansing time is soon upon you ♡ be
filled then with My Spirit of Love, so

13

that your sins will not suffocate you

ΙΧΘΥΣ ⊃Ð

20.1.92

Vassula, be on your guard; many claim they hear Me and are carrying projects but they are not Mine; they make plans, not inspired by Me; remember, you will be approached by those who do not consult Me; they rave with prophecies that are not pronounced by Me; you have already heard and seen it all; they announce month by month what will happen to you next; let them come

14

forward, do not be afraid; I shall cover you My child ♡

Later on:

Jesus, let Your Holy Face smile on us, and we shall revive. Our division devoured us like fire; since You alone perform marvels, bring us together, and let men renounce their folly; Your Plan is to unite us by unifying the date of Easter, thus bringing us reconciliation, I am calling for Your Divine Help.

My child, bear joyfully My Cross, praise the Father for His generosity; hear Me: the wicked may hope to destroy My Plan of Unity but they will be heading for their downfall; when I proposed Peace, universal Peace, nearly all were for war; how can I take up their

15

cause to defend them when My Father's Hand raises upon them? the net they have spread now will catch them inside ♡ what could I have done for all of you that I have not done? I have taken your faults on Myself, I have reconciled you to the Father, and My Life, I laid down for you, so what could I have done more that I have not done? — Vassula, of My Sacred Heart, rejoice Me and allow My Spirit in the inner room of your soul, allow My Spirit to breathe and dwell in the depths of your soul, leave Me free to

16

shatter all impurities and imperfections that confront Me; My Vassula, although your soul will leap like on fire every time I will lift My Hand to shatter all that still keeps you captive, do not fear, do not run away in horror, allow Me to uproot in your soul all these infirmities; I shall come like a tempest inside you and carry out the decision of My Heart, — and that is your preparation for our perfect union ♡ I had said in the beginning that you will be My Net and My Target, but then you had not understood the latter; you

17

had not understood that in order to prepare
you for this perfect union, I need to purify you
and adorn your soul; I would have to bend My
bow and set you as a target for My arrow,
oh what will I not do for you! no, it will
not be without wounds and torments, but then
do not fight away the Holy One; allow My Spirit
to augment in you, and My Divine Fire roar
in your soul; you will be molten under the
action of My Divine Fire, do not lament then
when I come to you like a hammer shattering
your imperfections, do not ask your Holy One

18

what is He doing? I am on My way to the
inner room, My dwelling place, and persistent
blocks will not stop Me from proceeding, I
shall burst them all with a tempest, I shall
devour these rivals;   O Lord go in moderation!
I want to bring to completion your purification,
therefore, do not restrain Me from proceeding,
you are so dear to Me, so let My Tenderness
envelop you, refuse Me nothing, soul; I want
to make out of you a docile instrument,
since My Presence will be felt inside you like
a fire, and like an arrow, do not fear, I

19

shall not break you, I shall only break My
rivals, I shall only be combating inside you;
I shall also be mindful of your frailty; I
have formed you and ordained you for this
mission to be My Echo, so allow your King to
rule over you, allow your Sovereign to reign
over you; nothing will escape My Eyes, every
little impurity will be sieged by My Purity
and annihilated, and My Light shall continue
to glow inside you, and My Spirit shall flow in
your spirit like a river ♡ so seek My Holy
Face untiringly and you will understand

20

that I Am is smiling on you ♡ ☧

peace be with you; hear Me, daughter: 20.1.92
have you looked around you? what have
you seen?

I have seen upheavels and even greater divisions
to come among us, before UNITY; I cannot
see the end of our struggle to unite, nor
the end of atheism.

My Soul, arbitrator of your generation, has
witnessed much more than upheavels,
divisions and atheism; I tell you, many
are plotting against Me, in My Own House
this very minute I hear them conspiring,

but soon, the islands will tremble on My Day, and although this generation will wail, I shall not listen, Heaven's door will be shut in that Day; and the earth naked, will groan like a widow, bereft in her sorrow; My Heart turns over inside Me and is sick already from the pitiful sound that will ring out from you, generation; indeed, I shall not be gloating over you, since I take no pleasure in abasing and afflicting the human race; once more there will be poured on you, but as never before My Holy Spirit, from a faint

flickering Flame, My Fire shall roar and renew you all; then, like a man entering a conquered city, I, the Lord, shall invade you with My Glory and ecclesia shall revive ♡ justice will prevail in the end; and you, daughter, do not fear to cry out for Me; do not be afraid of men, especially those who oppose you, be happy, daughter, I can read the innermost parts of these men and My jealous Ear overhears everything; they think they know everything, but they know nothing; daughter, I prayed for you to the Father, to consider

your frailty, Vassula, try and understand the Father; frail you are, but I have rooted you well inside Me, so that you may not swerve or sway when violent tempests come from time to time upon you; you are His offspring, and this is why out of His jealous Love and His Generosity He allows such oppositions; have you not heard how He renders through suffering, souls, to perfection and that suffering is part of your training? so be patient, daughter, be generous too and do not shudder and complain for nothing ♡ do not weary labouring, follow

the marks of My Blood I have left behind for Eternity, those who follow these marks will enter into My Kingdom; learn that the Father is not ruthless but ever so gentle with you; Wisdom loves you; therefore, daughter, observe the Commandments, live according to the Gospel, have Me as your Holy Companion and pray for My priests who represent Me ♡

24.1.92

During Holy Mass Jesus told me:

"This is only the beginning. You will see greater things than this."

This was said after I was praising Him for

25

His Wonders and His Works, since with His Power He opened the hearts of many in the World Council of Churches. The Lord had been preparing since summer messages about unity. Directives of His Desires. Then He allowed certain hearts in the W.C.C. to open and receive His Word, thus allowing me to go over to them in the week of unity to offer them Jesus' messages.

26. 1. 92

Vassula of My Sacred Heart, do you want to consecrate yourself entirely to Me?

yes, my Lord, I want.

then say these words:

Sacred Heart of Jesus,
come and invade me completely so that my motives will be Your Motives, my desires Your

26

Desires, my words Your Words, my thoughts Your Thoughts, then allow me to creep in the deepest place of Your Sacred Heart ♡ annihilate me altogether; I, Vassula, shall worship Your Sacred Heart from the core of mine, I promise to serve Your Sacred Heart with a fire inside me, I shall, with zeal, serve You more fervently than before; I am weak but I know that your Strength shall sustain me; do not allow me to lose sight of You, nor allow my heart to flutter elsewhere; I, Vassula, will look for Your

27

Sacred Heart alone and desire You alone;
        Sacred Heart of Jesus,
make me dislike all that is contrary to Your Holiness and to Your Will; sift me through and through and make sure that not one rival remains within me; from today, tighten the bonds of Love with which you have enlaced me, and make my soul thirst for You and my heart sick with love for You;
        Sacred Heart of Jesus,
do not wait, come and consume my whole

28

being with the Flames of Your ardent Love; whatever I will do from now on, will be done merely for Your Interests and Your Glory and nothing for me; I, Vassula, consecrate my life for you and from today, am willing to be the slave of Your Love, the victim of Your Burning Desires and of Your Passion, the benefit of Your Church, and the toy of Your Soul; make my traits resemble those of Your Crucifixion through the bitterness I will encounter in the deafness of souls, and to see them fall; give my soul its fill;

29

Sacred Heart of Jesus,

do not spare me from Your Cross, like the Father had not spared You; arrest my eyes, my thoughts and my desires to be captives of Your Sacred Heart; unworthy, I am, and I deserve nothing, but help me to live my act of consecration by being loyal, invoking Your Holy Name untiringly; make my spirit repulse all that is not You,

Sacred Heart of Jesus,

make my soul bear more than ever before, the Marks of Your Body for the conversion

30

of souls; I, Vassula, voluntarily submit my will to Your Will, now and forever; amen; and now My Spirit will rest in you ♡ .... Vassula, it pleases Me to see you spend your time for Me; all your sacrifices done in My Name do not go in vain; ΙΧΘΥΣ 🐟

27.1.92

peace be with you, little child; this grace has been given to you so that I, through you, will open the eyes of the blind and the ears of the deaf ♡ I will continue to manifest Myself through you, in this way; you

31

are a most imperfect instrument, but My Compassion sees your efforts in your imperfection and My Wrath gets disqualified by My Tenderness ♡ never doubt of My Love; I want weakness so that I may do everything;

it is I, Jesus

who shall give you* the directives

to Unity;

the hour has come for My Body to be glorified; men shall soon learn in which way I wish them to unite, My Way will not be their way .... now I have revealed

* To humanity

32

My desires to them, I have revealed My Heart to them; with My Power I shall unify the dates of Easter; it will not be forced upon you, I shall find a means with Peace; yes, with immense power I shall surprise you; today I have told them which course to take, and tomorrow I will lead them where I chose ♡ ΙΧΘΥΣ 🐟

Italy: Gera-Lario   30.1.92

Lord? I Am; am I to write what I have seen at dawn? write ♡

— I have seen Russia.

33

do not weep; she will recover; weep bitterly rather for those who have gone away from Me; I will rebuild her ♡ weep for the man who is dead; I will embellish her, Vassula;

O God, I have seen her misery! What I have seen is this: A woman approached me, young, not very beautiful but neither ugly. Her name: Russia. She came over to me and I noticed from her clothing that she was poor. — She opened her mouth to talk to me and I saw then that half of her teeth were missing. And that made her very ugly, but I knew that a woman, so young, would do something if half of her teeth were gone, unless extreme poverty covered her. Russia, in spite of her poverty and misery was courageous, and on her feet. She showed me her bread-giver, an old-fashioned instrument;* Russia was telling me that she will work on it, to be able to earn

* it looked like a weaving textile machine

34

whatever and keep alive. I was torn inside me with sadness. Then, another woman came, she was also Russia, she too, most of her teeth were missing. Then two more women came all of whom their teeth were partly missing too, showing extreme poverty*. Then, suddenly, a young man enters. He was the Husband of Russia. I noticed that He was well built, healthy, tall and very good looking.
— I thought: 'How could He stand someone like Russia, with no beauty in her, and repulsive for lack of teeth ... while I was thinking all these things, Russia's Husband approached her tenderly and put His Arm around her shoulders. And I saw in His Eye, Infinite Tenderness, Love and Fidelity for ever and ever. I saw that He would never abandon her in spite of her unattractiveness. — I recognized You, my Lord.

no, I shall not abandon her, nor does she repulse me; I am her Father and her Spouse,

* (Four women poverty stricken, does that mean four years of famine in Russia?)

35

and My Name is Faithful and True; I shall dress her up again giving her fine clothes, and her heart will be the ornament of a sweet and gentle disposition; I have never ceased to rain a downpour of blessings on her; I shall never deprive her of My Love; ah, Vassula, be patient as I am patient ♡ lean now on Me; ΙΧΘΥΣ ⋈

31. 1. 92

— No less than the height of heaven over earth is the greatness of Your love for those who fear You. (Ps. 103:11)

come and absorb all that is Me; absorb Love; I am Love, yet I suffer loneliness because of

36

the rejection of My Own; My children have forsaken the paths of Righteousness, the Fountain of Wisdom; they are not listening to Our Two Hearts, but it had been said that the Rebel, that is the spirit of Rebellion, who speaks words against the Most High and harasses the Saints of the Most High * will challenge My Power; this spirit of Rebellion considers changing seasons and My Law *², look around you only and you will understand; Rationalism and Modernism are the prime enemy of My Church because both of these lead

1+2 * Dn. 7:25

37

to atheism; both of them want to devour the whole earth, but, My daughter, I will breathe My Fire upon these renegades so that the scales from their eyes once fallen, they may see what great disorder they have produced and what oppression they had put upon Our Two Hearts ♡ I am going to pass through all of you;

repent!

for the Kingdom of Heaven is close at hand;

– come, write My next Message for all those

38

who will assemble to hear My Word in Nice;

(France)

peace be with you; My Return is imminent and My Face will be revealed from Heaven against all the impiety of the world; so be prepared; everyone who proved to be false will see what fatal wounds they have given to their soul; I will come among you in Splendour and in Glory; the Spirit of Truth will be revealed in you to cleanse your soul; you shall see Me face to face* and you

* That is: spirit with Spirit

39

shall see yourselves fully as you are known; so come to Me as you are now, do not wait to be saints, come and understand what I seek most from you; I love you with an everlasting Love, I have offered you My Life taking your faults on Myself, I have reconciled you to the Father and I allowed the hands that I Myself formed:

– to crucify Me –

so what could I have done more that I have not done? – if you say you love Me, take My Cross and follow Me and do not

40

look with consternation upon the other small crosses I place on your path; love has no limits, love endures with patience whatever comes, love is not resentful, but delights in the Truth and whatever the Truth offers; love is forgetful to calumnies said about you; so seek love, bless your enemies, I want you holy, but My beloved ones you are still so very far from perfection because the love of money is rooted deep inside this generation; dear children, do you really want to follow Me? then decide to follow My Footprints imbued still with

41

My Blood; do not fear, My Footprints will lead you to Me in your Abba's Arms; They will lead you to Him who held you first ♡ have confidence and rely on Our saving Love; I tell you:

in the end Our Two Hearts
will prevail ♡♡

take My Hand, daughter, do not fear, I shall take care of you; I Am is with you IXΘΥΣ ⤳

31. 1. 92

O Abba if Scriptures say: " Much hardship

42

has been made for man, a heavy yoke lies on the sons of Adam from the day they come out of their mother's womb, 'till the day they return to the mother of them all." (Si. 40:1)

Then my Lord You have said also to me in one of Your Messages for Our Heavenly Mother that She is the Second Eve, thus taking the place of Eve and what I discover again in Scriptures is that It confirms once more that Our Blessed Mother, Mary, is the Mother of all humanity.

daughter, you have given ear to Wisdom and My Own Heart is glad and My Soul rejoices when from your lips comes the Knowledge I have given you ♡ remain a nothing and allow Wisdom to instruct you; remain in My favour and do not fear the fiery wolves,

43

do not fear them My child * ♡

O Abba, You are shaken by terrible sights coming from us, Your children; godlessness, hatred, Satanism, abortions, greed for power even in the Church, injustice etc. and yet You came to me portraying the godless to save me from destruction; Your Graciousness which is a torrent of blessings came upon me. You offered me Your Friendship and became my Holy Companion and my Friend. Before the

Truth and Your
Covenant

you made me stand. O how bitter it is to feel Your Heart so sad, breathing in me Your Passion, uttering sighs of sorrows.

I am profoundly sad, daughter; but do not weep for Me, weep for your brothers and your

* Something between me and God.

44

sisters, because sin devours them like cancer; reserve your tears, daughter, for them. Vassula, your wounds are nothing compared to My Wounds; pray for them before My Finger touches the earth and melts it; I know you are delicate and faint but have I ever abandoned you? prophesy and reveal My Heart to all races and all nations ♡ aℵω.

6. 2. 92

daughter, I give you My Peace ♡ if anyone will ask you: " what is this all about ? " *

* God means the Messages.

45

answer: Compassion - and - Love is revealing Himself to mankind; Salvation leans all the way from Heaven to reach the Wretched, supplicating them to renounce their folly; what God is saying to us today means, Peace, Reconciliation and Love;

– Infinite Love –

1ΧΘΥΣ ⊰×⊱

11. 2. 92

Vassula, allow Me to use your hand, write:

peace be with you all; children, I tell you solemnly that the Real Light is already

46

on His way of Return; I am telling you this, My Own children, that you may all be ready to receive Me; the night of your era is soon over; understand how sins obscure the light in you; the love of this passing world is vile and could bring in you nothing, but darkness; but I tell you,

the night is almost over,
and your tripping or falling is soon coming to an end because the Power of My Holy Spirit will be in full union with you all, to guide you to live:

47

a True Life in Me, your God;

happy those who admit the Truth and live in accordance to the Truth; his room in heaven will not remain void for eternity but will be filled with his presence; I, Jesus, ask you to offer Me your heart and I shall place it into My Own Sacred Heart and revive it; I shall fragrance your heart and purify it; I shall fill your heart with My Light and My Warmth; I shall imbue your heart with My Love and I shall restore it entirely bringing it back to holiness; and with My

48

Divinity adorn it; – if you only realized what I am offering you, you would not hesitate or waver, to give Me all your heart, but you would listen to Me this time:

seek good and not evil,

pray with love

and do not judge;

soon My Light, like a Fire will pass through you to cleanse your soul from impurities; I shall enter My cities,* and shine in them; it will mean light not darkness; it will

* That is: our souls

49

be an overflow of Light; your cities* then
will be renewed and holy with My transcendent
Light, then .... the New Heavens and the
New Earth will come upon you and the
world of today will roll away like a scroll;
and like flowers that draw their life
from light, you too, My beloved ones, will
be inundated in My Light to revive; — can
flowers survive without any water? then why do
so many of you today refuse the flow of
My Holy Spirit and doubt that this Water

* That is : our souls

50

rising from My Throne is coming from Me?*
have you not read :

   'The Throne of God and of the
   Lamb will be in its place in
   the city; his servants will worship
   Him; they will see Him face
   to face and His Name will be
   written on their foreheads; It
   will never be night again and
   they will not need lamplight
   or sunlight, because the Lord God

* Ap. 22 : 1

51

      will be shining on them;'*[1]
have you not yet understood? My Spirit is
like a River and wherever this River flows,
everyone teeming in it,[2]* sick, lame, blind,[3]
all will be healed and will become witnesses of
the Most High; like fruit trees with leaves
that never wither and fruit that never
fails,*[4] you shall all be ; you will bear
fruit every month because this Water (My
Holy Spirit) comes from My Sanctuary*[5] in
which your spirit will make its Abode;

        *[2] Ez: 47:9
*[1] Ap. 22 : 3-5   *[3] spiritually   *[4] Ez. 47:12
  *[5] Ez: 47:12

52

I mean to deliver you from the clutches of
the Evil one and restore the memory of your
soul; I mean to open the hearts of stone, making
them utter from henceforth noble praises for Me
your God; — generation, do not say:
   "My wounds are incurable", and refuse
beforehand to be healed; do not say :
   "My Redeemer never listens to me";
today, your Redeemer says to you: the Tears
of Blood I shed over you year after year,
generation, testify My grief; I deprive no
one of My Mercy, so come to Me, fall into

53

My Arms and you will be healed; do not fear Me, I am an Inexhaustible Source of Love and Forgiveness; and you, you who say: " My Redeemer never listens to me;" I tell you: I am with you all the time and like a thirsty traveller I thirst for your words of love, I thirst for your prayers; invoke Me with your heart and I will reply; do not say:

"He is hiding His Face from me;" then look on the other side; I am watching every

54

single one of your steps and I never leave you from My Sight; I am with you all the time, but in your obscurity you fail to see Me, in your aridity you do not hear Me; turn your eyes upwards towards Heaven and search for Heavenly things, generation, and you will see My Glory;

it is for you to decide: My Heart is open for everyone to come and live inside It; be rooted in Me and you shall live; I bless you all, leaving the Sign of My Love on your foreheads; IΧΘΥΣ ⳨

55

13. 2. 92

Lord, is it fair to reduce the newly converted Greek prayer group into naught? Is it fair that they are chased away by one priest and dispersed to return into the desert they were once in?

Nassula, your priests need prayers !!

Lord, will You allow him to dry up a whole Vineyard? You have turned deserts into Rivers and arid ground into Springs of Water!

Nassula, your priests need prayers !

You have filled the starved with Your Fruits, Lord,
You satisfied the hungry,
You lifted the weary and
exalted the poor and the wretched,
You brought happiness to the suffering
and the sick were healed with Your Love
and those who were desperately
thirsty, You gave them Water,
Do not abandon them...

56

I shall not abandon them; My Nassula, your priests need prayers ... look, have faith in Me; ecclesia shall revive, My healing balm is:

LOVE

But there is no love among many of us!

I shall pour out My Spirit on all mankind, and make the heart of the inflexible melt and their iniquities will be purged in My Fire;

Lord, I will dare say one more thing: That little prayer group now is terrified by this priest as You know. I am not worthy myself, I am lost without You and the light inside me flickers almost to extinction without Your Light

57

your heart is set to tell Me more, finish your sentence, My daughter ♡

.... unity could not be built without the Greek orthodox priests; the sort of unity You desire does not please them.

yet My Vassula I have a list of generous men, they will be an example for the conversion of this generation; but have in mind this priest; honour My priests and offer Me sacrifices of reparation and I will solicit you with My favours ♡ resign yourself to Me and allow Me to test ♡ you now and then; I will heal all the disloyalty My Eyes witness A☧Ω

58

14.2.92

Vassula, peace be with you; let Me feel your love, resign yourself to Me, enter into My Heart and put into practise all that I have given you ♡

Lord, You showered me with blessings without the slightest merit. I am as You see in Your Hands, so do whatever You please with me.

live then for Me and console Me; be the sign of unity this generation rejects, yes, be the sign of unity coming from Me, and scorned and rejected from within your own House, from your people;* through you

* The Greek orthodox priests.

59

I display My Love for all nations, and through you I will continue to speak and point out how they reduced My Church to a desert; I offered your people a pact of Peace which can lead you all to brotherly unity; I have chosen you as a signpost for what unity will be like but they do not listen; they do not bend either; instead they run to offer Me incense, but what am I to do with all their incense? I want incense from their heart, I want peace

* The Greek orthodox priests

60

from their heart, I want praises from their heart, I want love, mercy and compassion from their heart;

I want reconciliation from their heart;

ah, daughter, do not weary crossing this desert, your Redeemer is near you and we are bonded together; I have posted you for this mission to flash like lightning My Words to all nations; — tell them that if they say to be witnesses of the Most High let them then show Me their peace through integrity

61

and honour through devotedness; tell them
to examine their path and return to Me,
and I shall give them the Spirit of understanding ♡   today I am offering them
Mercy in a time of trouble; I am offering
them Compassion in their appalling misery;
I am giving them the Gift of My Love;
    repeatedly I have been stretching out My
Hand to lift them to Me, and yet how
often have they responded? I have been showing them My pity and My Compassion; how
long am I to allow them to rock Me with

62

sorrow by rejecting to do My Will?
must I still hold back the Father's
Hand? the Father's Justice is flaring up
already to light up the crimes of this
world .... I poured out from babe's mouths
My bitter supplications, for
        peace and reconciliation among brothers,
but look how My supplications were received .... ah, My daughter, be the defender
                of the Truth,
lay your head on My Heart and when
    you will hear the sound of My

63

Heart-beats your courage will return to
you;   do not give in to the promptings
of your weaknesses, trust Me, trust Me;
.... look*, courage daughter, I am by your
side and so long as I am by your side,
you will be kept on your feet; .... daughter?
I shall never abandon you .... ♡ listen,
hear Me Vassula, I am sharing ♡ My Cross
with you; look, My Vassula, My Love is
before your eyes and My Loyalty surrounds
you;   whenever I see from far off an anger

* I felt Jesus was trying to uplift my spirit.

64

from a legion of demons heading towards you
to strike you and hurl themselves on you to
tear you to pieces, I come between you and
them, leaving them trembling; console then
your heart in My Heart and do not fear,
courage! no demons will be allowed to
strike you nor will I allow them in their
fierce rage to leap on you and burn you;
I am standing near you to give you
signals when to open your mouth to
speak in My Name ♡ come the Light
is your Companion; IXθΥΣ ><>

1

18.2.92

Lord, I will not let my eyes off You, lest I fall again in apostasy.

Allow me to worship You at Your Footstool. O Lord, display now Your Power on us all. Bring upon us all Your Tempest that will whirl away our sins.

Let Your Fire (the Holy Spirit) come upon us to enliven us and purify us. It is hard to cross this treacherous desert in the dark.

Maranatha! Come!

peace My beloved, do not be in terror, My decision has been taken, I shall ravage the earth with My Purifying Fire and I shall carry out My Plan sooner than foreseen, the time of waiting is soon over ♡ as for you, My child,

2

do not be intimidated by Folly; turn your eyes towards Me and lean on Me, I am Your Strength; – look! pray for your priests *, pray that they may turn to Me and draw from Me: Resourcefulness, Peace, and Love; many are decaying and very fast too; pray for those *¹ who play havoc with My blossoming flowers *²; tell your priests * that if among them there are a few who are still alive, it is due to

* The Greek Orthodox priests
*² The newly converted Greek youth. Converted through our Lord's messages.

3

My Tears; I water their faith with My Tears, so I weep in agony to keep this remnant alive; My Church is crumbling like rotten wood and all I hear from them is:

"Is there a drought?"

they flout piety, they list bitter accusations against the Works of My Holy Spirit and allow their mouth to condemn them! the hour of darkness brought the Hour of Adoration to nil; worse still, they have established a monopoly of ostentation and presumption; I, their Lord, stand before

4

them and ask them: "Why do you scorn the consolation that I give to My children today through the smallest part of My Church?" – the Heavens will wear away soon and you are still unaware and in deep sleep; I shall come to you like a thief without telling you at what hour to expect Me,* I am asking you now with Tears in My Eyes, tell Me: What happened to My flock? where are My perennial pastures? why are My sons and daughters in captivity? where is the

* Ap. 3:3

5

youth of today? why has the fragrance I
had given you turned into a stench?
— I weep over you — I weep over your excessive
pride.... your excessive pride made My Church
resemble a gaping grave; but you too will
be subdued; My Fire is close now; I will
bring you down from your glory .... and when
you will ask: " what happened? " I will
tell you then: " My Kingdom has been taken
from you and given to a people who will
now produce its fruit," *   it is the Spirit

* Mtt. 21: 43

6

who gives life, surely you have enough respect
for My Holy Spirit? then why do you
offend My Holy Spirit by persecuting Him?
judge for yourselves what I am saying;
why are your young people separating from
Mother Church to follow a second-rate philosophy? you have done well in remembering
My Holy Spirit so constantly and in main-
taining the traditions just as I passed
them on to you, however, you speak without love and you are blinded by your zeal!
you have lost the insights of My Mysteries

7

because of your zeal! have you not read:
' there is a remnant, chosen by grace; by
grace, you notice, nothing therefore to do
with good deeds, or grace would not be
grace at all!' (Rm. 11: 5-6)   I love you
all but it is not without suffering, because you are objecting to My Holy Spirit's
gifts; you are not objecting to a human
authority, but to Me your God ♡ I am
reminding you of one last thing: one
day you will see Me face to face and I
will ask you to give Me an account of

8

the way you looked after the souls I had
entrusted you with; today still you are
making Me out to be a liar because you do
not believe anymore the testimony I had
given you all about the Reminder of My
Word :
            My Holy Spirit;
wash your hearts clean and the heavens will
shine on you; from above, I have been watching you, City of Tradition, you have
practised the exact observances of the Law
of My Primitive Church, but today you are

9

blinded by ostentation and pay little attention or none at all to the weightier matters
of My Law - Mercy! Love! Humility!
            and a spirit of Forgiveness ....
My sorrow is great and I groan inwardly as
I wait for you to seek for the greater gifts
of My Spirit; I am weary of seeing you
preach spiritual things unspiritually; had
they understood the depths and the weightier matters of My Spirit today they would
have accepted the gifts too of My
Spirit, but the pride that you take in

10

yourselves is incessantly lacerating Me ♡ I
have entrusted you with thousands of souls
to teach and help them gently, drawing
them into My Heart, reminding them of
My Tenderness, My Love and My great
thirst for them, but you pass premature
judgement on them and load them with
burdens that are unendurable, burdens that
you yourselves do not move a finger to lift!
in My days I was the stumbling block
and today My Holy Spirit is again,
            - the stumbling block -

11

for many of My sacerdotal souls ♡ - the
Eyes of the Lord, I am telling you are
not only turned towards the righteous and
the virtuous, My Eyes also turn towards the
wretched and the ones you call unworthy;
the stars from the sky will soon drop
to the earth and the powers of heaven
will shake and you will still be unaware;
this earth will soon disappear and the new
heavens and the new earth will be upon you
and you will still be running away from
My Spirit ♡, yet, if even today you

12

humble yourselves and sincerely admit you are
sinners and unworthy, I shall take away
the spirit of lethargy that is hovering over
your nation! you say yourselves 'rich',
show Me your riches then; 'famine'
is the only word I hear from your country;
'famine' is written all over you; if you
say yourselves rich, then where are your
glorious pastures? why do I stumble on decaying corpses? how is it I hear no sound
from you? - My Holy Spirit in His
Infinite Mercy descends now to feed you

13

all and fill your spirit with My Celestial Manna; as a Shepherd I shall look for My strayed sheep, I shall tend their wounds with everlasting Love, I will support the weak and the weary and those you pasture no more; I will console My children; so do not hinder Me or become an obstacle in these days of Mercy; do not contradict what you teach on My Spirit; I have told you all this now before My Day comes; will I hear: " God, here I am! I am coming to repent! I will stop insulting

14

Your Spirit of Grace because I know that if I do, I would be severely punished; " it is for your salvation that I speak and if I reproach you it is because of the

greatness of the Love I have for you;

IXΘYΣ 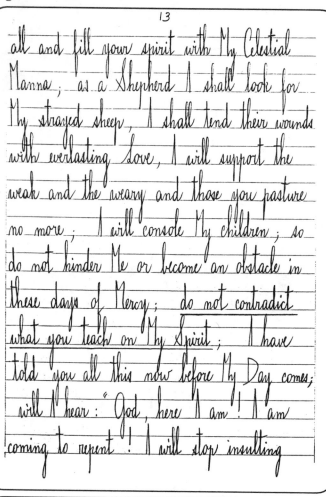 Vassula, pray for your priests to learn real humility from Me ♡

March, 92

Satan could have easily killed me this morning. While I was dusting a glass-shelf with icons and religious objects on it, it fell breaking the lower shelf too. I saw big pointed blades falling all around me and all the way out of that room in the entrance hall. When it stopped I waited in silence to see where the blood will trickle.

15

I had nothing, not even a scratch. Normally I should have been sliced from my stomach all the way to my feet.
Later on:

My Vassula, let Me lead you step by step; stay small My flower and lean on your Saviour; I love you, child, Satan desperately tries to lay a hand on you and lame you; * not only does he use people to gather false accusations against you, but in his anger, he will use even the law of nature to turn against you; but I am your Devout Keeper

* I understood it spiritually.

16

and your Shelter, so do not fear, My Eyes are upon you incessantly; hide always in My Sacred Heart ♡ come, we shall continue to pursue souls for their salvation; I shall lead you, My beloved, everywhere on earth and wherever I pass through I will leave a trace of the subtlest odours behind Me, I will spread My fragrance of myrrh from soul to soul to ravish their hearts; delight your Saviour, flower, and allow Me to use you progressively, I shall not break you nor will I wrench from you your liberty; let

17

your heart remain captive of My Love, though
without tiring of Me; I am your Beloved
Companion who have given you a Treasure:
I have given you the

Gift of My Love;
I shall give you My Strength and My
Patience; flower, My Spirit rests on you to
guide you and remind you of My Teachings so
be generous and offer your time to germinate
this earth; have reverence always for Me; am
I not your sole love? am I not the
King of Kings? work hard with Me and

18

contrary to what you think, most of your
efforts are not futile, My Power gives them a
Divinity that reaches their aim; if the Tempter whispers in your ear telling you that your
words are ineffectual, I tell you, My child,
do not listen to him; I shall continue to
pour out My Heart on you all and descend
untiringly from Heaven to nourish the
hungry, satisfying every taste; I shall
continue to expose My Sacred Heart and
demonstrate My Tenderness towards everyone
whosoever will eat Me and drink Me will

19

be transformed to live a
true life in Me, your God;
whosoever will turn towards Me will be saved;
by just one look at Me and I will transfigure you; — daughter remain unnoticed
and nothing, remain hidden by your help-
lessness by your frailty so that My Bounty
and My Power may spread even more now;
the sowing is not finished and the whole
world will soon echo with My Voice;
daughter, you are very precious to Me and I
love you to tears, I love you all to tears;

20

and from Heaven My Lips moistened with
Grace bring to all of you My Message of
Peace; from all Eternity I have loved you
and blessed you; and from your crib I had
watched over you and defended you. I know
how misery enwrapped you all to total blind-
ness; seek Me and I shall give you light;
I will give you life again and make your
soul long for all that is Holy, therefore,
daughter, continue to seek My Holiness and
My Perfection; bless Me and praise Me;
sow when I sow, sow abundantly and

21

wherever I take you to sow, soon you
shall pass this era's threshold to enter into
an Eternal Peace ♡ endure in the meantime all
that I endure, alone you are not; persevere,
My child, and remember Who is near you

blessing you; Love loves you, ΙΧΘΥΣ 🐟

— In my times of persecutions-3. 3. 92
Lord, I have not spoken in secret, all I say
is in prayer and in Your Assembly praising You.
I am trying to obey Your Sacred Heart, and the
Instructions I received from You, I do my best to
display them as they were given me. Although
I am poor and can hardly give You anything,
I have given You the only thing I have and
You have told me is mine, I have offered Your
Majesty: my will, that You may use it if
it pleases You, for Your Merciful Designs.

22

I know, My child, but have they not also hated
Me for no reason? anyone who issues from Me to
witness for the Truth will be hated, persecuted
and hunted like game — a servant is not
greater than His Master .... these persecutors
would be blameless in the Father's Eyes if
they had not known My Law, but as it is
they have seen My Law, yet only in darkness;
they call themselves doctors of the Law and
believe they know everything but in reality
they know nothing; they think by judging
you and condemning you in public that they

23

are doing a very holy duty for Me, your God;
had they followed My Commandments and kept
them they would not have judged; had
they any love in them they would have kept
My Words and My Law; but in reality
they are not judging you, they are judging
My Good Works on you all; I have
only commissioned you to go out and be My
Echo, in being My Echo I expect you to
bear fruit, fruit that will last .... — but
they have not understood .... My child, continue
to do the work I have commissioned you for:

24

bring souls to Me, that I may consume them
in My Sacred Heart; I am thirsty for souls;
listen, the evidence of My Holy Works are
shining on you all to take away this darkness;
the evidence of My Holy Works are their good
fruit, fruit that lasts; the evidence of My
Holy Works is the gift of Peace I am giving
you and the Love I am infusing you with;
the evidence of My Holy Works is My salvation calls to the

Eucharistic life;
the Father and I want true worshippers,

25

worshippers who will worship in spirit and truth ♡ My Spirit of Truth descends all the way to your doorstep to remind you that in the end

— Our Two Hearts will prevail —

this is to fulfil the words written in Scriptures: 'after the three and-a-half days, God breathed life into them and they stood up', (Ap. 11:11) yes, in all Glory, for, 'these are the Two Anointed Ones' (Zc. 4:14) who stand side by side; Our Two Hearts are like 'Two Olive Trees, one to the right and one to the left', (Zc. 4:3)

26

My Sacred Heart has fathomless Riches and many things to say to you all, My little children;

I am the Resurrection and the Life,

I come to resurrect your devotion to My Sacred Heart and the Immaculate Heart of your Mother, so do not fear, stay on your guard, for many will come using My Name manipulated by the Evil One, to deceive you and blow away the little flame left in you and leave you in total darkness; many will fall away because their roots were not in Me; pray that you may not be tempted by the Evil

27

one; alas for you who continue to persecute My mouthpieces saying: we would never have joined in shedding the blood of the prophets, had we lived in our fathers' day; I tell you, all of this will recoil on your heads unless you repent! My beloved children, the burglar comes by night * so stay awake and do not allow him to break in your house; be in constant prayer to Me; to pray without ceasing is to be aware of My Presence before you; to be aware of My Presence is to be awake, to be awake is to be with light and be sound; your

* That means Satan comes in a dark soul much easier.

28

house is your soul; see to it then that the light inside you is not darkness; do not let the Tempter find you asleep ♡ you are My friends, remember? love one another as I love you, anything you will ask in My Name I shall give you; some of you today are sad because the world is passing premature judgement on My Sacred Heart and the Immaculate Heart of your Mother, but soon Our Two Hearts will show the world how wrong it was, about judging when I will reveal My Holy Face * in

* That is in the Purification Day, when we will see our sins with God's Eyes.

29

them; daughter, write: 'when I will break the sixth seal) there will be a violent earthquake and the sun will go as black as coarse sackcloth; the moon will turn red as blood all over, and the stars of the sky will fall on to the earth like figs dropping from a fig-tree when a high wind shakes it; the sky will disappear like a scroll rolling up and all the mountains and islands will shake from their places; then all the earthly rulers, the governors and the commanders, the rich people and the men of influence, the

30

whole population, slaves and citizens, will take to the mountains to hide in caves and among the rocks; they will say to the mountains and the rocks, 'Fall on us and hide us away from the One who sits on the Throne and from the anger of the

Lamb; *

for the Great Day of My Purification is soon upon you and who will be able to survive it?

* Ap. 6: 12-17 Here Jesus indicates plainly, that in the day of purification, everyone in the world will experience his state of his soul and again everyone will recognize the Lamb, meaning Jesus

31

everyone on this earth will have to be purified, everyone will hear My Voice and recognize Me as the Lamb; all races and all religions will see Me in their interior darkness, this will be given to everyone like a secret revelation to reveal the obscurity of your soul; when you will see your insides in this state of grace you will indeed ask the mountains and the rocks to fall on you; the darkness of your soul will appear as such that you would think the sun lost its light and that the moon too turned into blood; this is how your soul

32

will appear to you, but in the end, you will only praise Me; — if a stranger comes your way and tells you that the food * I have been giving you is vile, do not listen to him, listen to the language of My Sacred Heart, the language of My Cross; let your fidelity to My Sacred Heart bloom once more, consecrate yourselves all to My Sacred Heart and the Immaculate Heart of your Mother ♡ I will be visiting you again, My little ♡ children; so courage My friends; you are hounded

* These messages

33

but it is only by the world; you are
insulted for My sake? rejoice! for I was
too; you are treated as the offal of the world
because you love Me? I bless you and join
you in your sufferings; you are the jest of
your people? but so was I, your King;
you are not more than Me your Master;
My secret intentions are revealed now, in
your dormant times; the revelation of My
Sacred Heart is revealed in these end of
Times again to awaken your hearts and bring
you all back fervently to this Devotion; so

34

among you there must be no premature
judgement; love Me and bless Me; I am
always with you and I will continue to
reveal the Riches of My Sacred Heart in each
one of you ♡
Vassula, ♡ My child, I shall strengthen your
stem and replace the petals your accusers
ripped from you to give you this joy I feel
whenever you offer Me your will ♡
Love loves you IXΘYΣ ⤳

35

4. 3. 92

I am listening Lord, now.
My child, listen and write: I am Boundless
Tenderness and Compassion, but My people heap
in My Church one betrayal on another, am I
to keep silent? My Body, from the sole of My
Foot to My Head hurts and is in great agony;
I have got impressive wounds and I am taunted
by My Own; a great and innumerable multitude
is on its way to perdition; many of My
sacerdotal souls flout piety; I pronounced
warnings since the Time of Fatima to this day,
I have emptied My Heart on you, generation,

36

but many of you have forgotten the ransom
that was paid to free you....* Vassula, you
are not listening as I want you to listen ....*²
for the sake of My Love, child, speak to Me!
do not lack courage, I love you!

Lord my persecutors are now putting in print
something against me.

they are My persecutors too, not yours only,
but I tell you they will quite certainly destroy
themselves by their own work of destruction if
you do not pray for them and their reward

* Jesus suddenly stopped, *² Jesus changed tone, like
He was pleading.

37

will be evil for the evil they are doing; My Heart is a vast ocean of Love and Forgiveness;

I Know Lord, but they tempt back the ones who have only just escaped from the Evil one.

daughter, Wisdom has given you a gift, to hear, write and understand Love's Desires; these points, daughter, are not easy to understand by unspiritual people; they will never accept anything of My Spirit; they see it all as nonsense; they will go on teaching with the current of the world, like philosophy is taught; then, have you not read that the spiritual gifts from My

38

Holy Spirit will be hard to understand so long as they think and come to Me like philosophers? have you not read that these are the points that these people distort as long as they are not in the Spirit, in the same way as they distort the rest of Scripture? Scripture has warned you all about these people; believe and grow in the grace I have given you, soon My Purifying Fire will come upon you all to dissolve in flames the crimes of this world ♡

your Holy Mother and I have emptied Our Hearts to you all since the day of

39

Fatima, but My observances that I desire from you are not carried out and only a remnant are listening; this generation is deceiving itself, they have broken all My Commandments, how can I not come to you by Fire and thunder you as I thundered Sodom and Gomorrah?

Because maybe we are more than ten Lord? (There was some silence)

.... you stupefy Me! you stupefy Me because I had started to believe your lips would never dare utter Abraham's bargain ♡ I have been

40

provoking you to utter cries of mercy before the deadly hour comes, I have been provoking you to offer Me prayers, but they are not sufficient....

What must I do Lord?
I am all day with You, working for You and serving Your Interests.
You are my Life, my Breath in this exile. I know I am a wretch and sinning as much as I breathe, yet, You came to me and lifted my soul to You to taste Your Sweet Knowledge as Your disciples tasted it.
You have revived my heart and turned my ear towards Your Sacred Heart.
Your Mighty Hand caressed my head and made my heart since then sing praises to You. I suffer loneliness and excruciating agonies to rip one's heart when from time to time

41

*You turn away Your Holy Face
from me, leaving my soul alone in
the Dark Night,
but I am dragging on, because:
I love You to madness.*

Vassula of My Sacred Heart, I have raised you
to drive My Church into Unity

(Jesus said this very calmly.)

- I have raised you to appease the Father's
  Justice;

- I have raised you to embellish My Church;
I have allowed you to step into My Hall to
glorify Me; I have courted you to love Me; I
have taken you out of the land of Egypt to

42

thrust you out as one thrusts a net to catch
souls for Me; you are to relent the Father's
Justice by adoring Me, by praying, by penance,
sacrifice, fasting and by reducing your size
you have no merits but your humble plea
can reach the Father; will you drink now
from the same cup that the Father has given
Me? .... do not fear, there is not much
left in it now, I have been letting you sip
from it now and then, daughter, I have
been drawing your head towards My Cup,
delicately, so do not move back now with

43

disdain, love what I love ♡ do not be afraid
and do not ever imagine ♥ that I am going
to lead you to Me without My Cross; be concerned
on what I am concerned; ask Me to cure the
rest of you; ask My graces; ask My blessings....
ask the Father to relent;

*Ask the Father to relent .... we are at the verge of
a destructive fire*
shsh .... ask the Father to relent,* that is why
I am continually welcoming you to pray; and
about the wicked accusations that are being
circulated against you, do not fear; be at

* Jesus said these words very softly giving me so much to
hope for.

44

peace and do not give way to sadness; I have
called you for the revival of My Church and
I will not fail you; pray constantly; be
patient till the end ♡ My Day is very near
and I will come like a thief in the night;
this is why, My child, Satan together with
the beast* are incessantly attacking all those
who come from Me and making war against
My mouthpieces, but in the end they*² will
be defeated ♡ the devil has gone down to you
in a rage together with the beast, but
Love will conquer evil.— Canada is Mine;

* That is: freemasonry (see Ap. 13) *² Satan and the
beast

45

the beast* could make virulent sounds to cover My Voice in this country because it knows that they are the people My Sacred Heart loves, but I, the Lord, <u>will stay there</u>, and I tell you, that all evil spirits roaming in that nation are already fearing at the sound of My Footsteps and at the sound of My Sacred Heart; My Holy Spirit will not shun from the beast nor from those who have been convinced by it; I will expand even more now My graces, for no angel, no prince, nothing that exists, nothing still to come, not any

* Freemasonry

46

power, or height or depth, nor any created thing, can ever come between you and My Love;¹ no one will be able to stop the outpouring of My Holy Spirit ♡ I am sending you to them*² to remind ♡ them all of the greatness of My Love; I will give you enough resources to hold your ground ♡ Love is with you ♡ IΧΘΥΣ ><>

(Message, call to unity)   27. 3. 92

My Vassula, write: dear friends, dear companions, dear brothers, there is no

*¹ Rm. 8: 35-39   *² That is: the Canadians

47

such love as Mine; what have you done with My Love? My brothers, be united by following the rules of My Heart which are Love and Humility; the things you think to unite are earthly things and they will not bring you to unity, they can do nothing and offer nothing; but many of you have become slaves of your minds; so long as you do not reconcile in humility with each other and love one another as I love you, your separation will remain; My children, must I

48

go through the pain again this Easter season*¹? many of you have seen the dumb speaking, the lame walking and the blind with their sight, but yet you continue to praise Me only with your lips; I tell you truly, as I once said: 'anyone who blasphemes against My Holy Spirit will not be forgiven;*² by persecuting My Holy Spirit you are hardening your hearts, and if your hearts are hardened by the lure of sin, all that is wicked will not be seen by you,*³

*¹ By having the Feast of Easter separated;
*² Lk. 12: 10   *³ One cannot, in this state, recognize their evil and so cannot REPENT to be forgiven.

49

thus you will bring condemnation upon you and judgement without mercy, as you have not been merciful ♡ I watch from above all of you, each one of you; I tell you, whoever continues to work for his own interests and his own glorification has already lost My Heart; their convictions are not My convictions for in their minds they are the same as Satan; rivalry and competition for earthly power devours their minds, egoism and pride have already condemned them; all these earthly things will make them

* Jesus talks about these people to me.

50

perish by their very use! seldom do I hear their prayers; today, you are surrounded by false teachers*¹ who openly and without fear stand before Me and proclaim Satan's knowledge that is based on a lie; they disown My Divinity by disowning My Resurrection*²; pray for these false teachers that they may escape damnation! and I tell each one of you now:

'anyone who claims to be in the light but hates

* the modernists. *² This is also why the Holy Shroud disturbs them so much!

51

his brother is still in the dark;*¹

whoever believes in his state of darkness that he is glorifying Me, believes in he who first tempted your parents*²; — I have been giving you signs, but you do not believe in My signs because your voices are drowning My Voice that speaks through My mouthpieces; the night will soon be with you and many will taste death because you were never grounded in the truth but were

*¹ 1 Jn 2:9   *² Adam & Eve

52

based on lies, I come to you through these signs to open your eyes and heal you, yet when I tell you the truth and tell you that it is I, the One whom you say, ' He is your Lord' that speaks to you, you turn away giving your ear to Satan so that he may use you; no, you do not understand My Language not more than you understand My wonders, because you have preferred the devil; whatever I say or ask does not penetrate in you since you have lost the sense of the

53

language of My Spirit; I am thirsty
for your salvation, I am thirsty to share
My Kingdom with you, I am thirsty for
you to reconcile with each other so that you
may truly say: I am reconciled with
God ♡ your division is a sin and
no one can claim to be righteous when from
his lips he discredits not only his brothers,
but the leader of them all*; justice,
mercy, good faith! these you should

* The Pope.

54

have practised without neglecting the other parts
of My Law; and you, you who delight
in your division and swear by My Throne
and by Me, I, who sit on it, I tell you
as I have said once:

'you are like whitewashed tombs
that look handsome on the
outside, but inside are full of
dead men's bones and every kind
of corruption'
how can you believe you can escape
damnation? you fail to please Me and

55

your corpses litter this desert you are living
in; by sinning in your division against
each other, it is I,
                    the Lamb,
against whom you sin, this sin of your
division which massacres daily My Body;
it is I, the Lamb whom you lead by
force and by your own law to be recrucified; it is My Body you are
mutilating and bruising,
          I Am the Victim;
can you not see? can you not see

56

that you are in communion with demons?
can you not see with whom you are
sharing at your table? how can I
rejoice when all I see are demons at
table with you? so long as you rejoice
in your division, you are under Satan's
power who without ceasing is anointing with
a lie those who rejoice in their division;
each one of you is looking to one another
for approval of these messages of unity
and are not concerned that this Easter
My Body again will go through

57

excruciating pains <u>because</u> of your division; believe that I am Me, do not be the slaves of your mind, come to Me as long as the day lasts, soon the night will envelop this world; I have asked to see you*² and talk to you, and so I did, for it is on account of uniting you that I have prompted you with My Messages of Unity ♡ but how hard it is for those who ♡ are slaves of their mind

*¹ Christ suffers mystically.
*² All those who invited me to give the messages of unity and talk to them in the World Council of Churches in Geneva.

58

to enter into the Mysteries of Wisdom! how hard it is for the rich in spirit to enter into My Kingdom! I tell you: many who are first will be last, and the last first; My child, be My Heaven by devoting yourself to Me, I am with you; IXΘΥΣ ⊂><

30. 3. 9

All day long I desire you my God, all day long I pine away with love for You, because of Your Tenderness and Your Infinite Mercy, my God; Your Love that You showed me makes my soul cry out more than ever to You to rescue me. I long for the House You live.

59

I long for Your Sacred Court. So tell me my Lord and God, what can I expect? will You reconsider my frailty? Ah, free me from all my sins and reconsider me. All my hopes are in You my God. Amen.

Ah My Vassula, be My consoling instrument; I, Jesus bless you; fear not, My child, I am the All Faithful and by your side; My child, for the sake of My Love I have tested your faith and I found My glorification; I am no stranger for you so allow Me to draw you one more time inside My Wounds, do not fear,

60

I will show My glory through you and men will learn how I suffered; come, approach Me, My Fire of Love is flaming out of My Sacred Heart and if you allow Me, I will visit you in this way and make a vivid torch out of you; you are destined to honour Me and lead souls to Me so that I may consume them; I will make vessels of light out of them, brilliant flames that never cease, that never dim and that can never be snuffed; ah My little one, every fibre of My

61

Heart cries out for Love! Peace! Unity!
I am your Holy Companion, creation,
your most Faithful Friend who invites you
night and day at My table; I
appeal for your friendship without ceasing,
to save you .... My Father has reserved
a Fire for the sins of this generation
and like a gale it will come suddenly
upon you; people say: ' we will have
peace ' even when their heart is for war
against Me and the powers of heaven; like
a gust of wind I shall come to pronounce

62

sentence on this godless generation, like
a hurricane I shall blow on you and
scatter you like chaff;

Lord, what about those who love You?
what about Your victim souls? surely
there must be a few men who love You?
There are a few, my King, who have not
abandoned you to serve false gods or the
beast.

put them on a scale .... and see which
of the two the weightier part; to
this day many do not feel neither contri-
tion nor fear; I am willing to give you
all, My Mercy before My Justice and I am

63

willing to give everyone a single heart
with a spirit of Love in them, but I
need more victim souls, I need sacrificial love; how many are ready to
sacrifice? how many are ready to
offer themselves to Me to turn them into
crucifixes? will the ear of anyone
yield to My supplications? how many
are willing to become peacemakers and
sow seeds which will bear fruit in
purity? who can remain uncontamina-
ted by the world until My return?

64

who will be quick to listen? I am
kind and ever so compassionate but very
few want to be in union with Me;
who will give away his motives for My Motives? who is willing to give up his interests for Mine? who will seek what
is least sought in this world and
bear It with love?

– My Cross –

and who is ready to seek what is least
sought among you, who will seek: Love?
come, pray for the conversion of the world ♡

ΙΧΘΥΣ ⟩⊂○